PRICELESS!

SEE PEOPLE DIFFERENTLY
LEAD PEOPLE BETTER

Scott Doggett

Publisher:
National Academy of Leadership Development, LLC
www.NationalALD.com

ISBNs:
Paperback: 979-8-9992968-0-1
Hardcover: 979-8-9992968-1-8
eBook: 979-8-9992968-2-5
Printed in the United States of America
U.S. Copyright Registration Pending

Table of Contents

Dedication

To the leaders and misfits who taught me what to do...

and what not to.

To the mentors who believed in me before I did.

To my family and friends, who fill my life with purpose and joy.

To God who gave me this voice...

and the courage to use it.

To every person I've been blessed to lead –

Thank you for shaping me as much as I hoped to shape you.

And to every person who's ever doubted their worth:

You are seen.

You are valued.

You are priceless.

This is for you.

Introduction: Why This Book, Why Now

We are in a leadership crisis – but not the kind you see on the news. This crisis is quieter. Closer. It's the kind that leaves people feeling invisible, questioning their value, and wondering if leadership even sees them. You can feel it in the broken trust between managers and teams, the revolving door of disengaged employees, and the slow erosion of purpose in people who used to love what they do. At the heart of it is something simple, yet often overlooked:

We've forgotten how to see people.

This book was born from decades of watching what happens when leaders treat people like numbers – and what happens when they don't. I've worked in hotels and resorts, corporate boardrooms, nonprofits, and training classrooms. And the one leadership truth that has never failed is this:

People who feel valued, act valuable.

But it's more than that. It's not just about making people feel good...it's about leading in a way that honors their humanity. Their story. Their self-worth. And for me, that conviction is rooted in my personal faith. As a Christian, I look to Jesus as the ultimate model of servant leadership – not because He held power, but because He gave it away in service of others. This book isn't a sermon. It's not here to convert you. But I'd be dishonest if I didn't share the source of the values I've tried to live and lead by. Whether you share my faith or not, I hope you'll see something beautiful in this way of leading – something that transcends profit and position and points us back to purpose.

This book is for anyone who wants to lead with more courage, clarity, and compassion. Whether you're an executive, a team leader, or just someone others look to for guidance – you are influencing people every day. And the way you treat those people has a ripple effect that lasts much longer than you may realize.

You'll find stories in here – some uplifting, some heartbreaking. All of them are real. And throughout the book, you'll come across special stories titled:

"What Were They Thinking?"

These are snapshots of real leadership moments submitted by people across industries and backgrounds. After each one, you'll be invited to pause and reflect:

1. What was the person thinking at this moment?

2. How did this affect their feelings and emotions?

3. What impact did this have on their behavior and performance?

You'll find the actual reflections from the people who lived those stories in the Appendix at the back of the book. My hope is that this format sharpens your empathy and helps you recognize these moments in your own leadership.

You'll also find:

*   A simple but powerful *Priceless Leadership Model* that explains how people interpret and react to leadership behaviors

*   The *Service-Profit Chain*, a research-based case for why putting employees first leads to better business outcomes[3]

- A *Priceless Leadership Assessment* tool to help you identify your strengths and growth areas

- Key takeaways, reflection questions, mini-challenges, and a little humor at the end of each chapter to turn insights into action and to have some fun!

This isn't just a book to read...it's a journey to walk. It's a mirror to hold up. And it's a practical guide to leading like people matter.

Because they do.

And if enough of us lead like they do... we just might change the world.

Let's begin.

Part I:

THE FOUNDATION

Before we dive in, take a breath. Whether you're reading this from the corner office, your kitchen table, or the breakroom between meetings – know this: this book isn't just about leadership.

It's about people.

It's about how we see them. How we shape them. How our influence either lifts them up or slowly wears them down.

In this first section, we'll uncover what leadership is truly built upon – not titles or tactics, but something deeper: *the heart.*

Because if leadership is anything, it's personal.

And the most meaningful change always begins within.

"The way we see people is the way we treat people, and the way we treat people is the way they become." — *Johann Wolfgang von Goethe*

Chapter 1

Leadership Is a Heart Issue
Why people-first leadership matters more than ever.

One of my favorite questions to ask during leadership work-shops is this: "*Who was the best leader you've ever had – and who was the worst? And why?*" That question never fails to stir something up. Within seconds, people start nodding, smiling, cringing, or even tearing up. Because whether you've been in the workforce for two years or twenty, you've likely encoun-tered both ends of the leadership spectrum: the kind of leader who makes you want to show up early and stay late, and the kind who makes you question why you show up at all.

I've experienced both.

Let's start with the worst.

Years ago, I was a young General Manager of a hotel in Connect-icut. I was proud of the team we were building. We had momen-tum. Energy. People were starting to believe that work could feel like purpose. But my boss? He didn't believe in all that. His man-agement philosophy was, to put it kindly, outdated.

During one of his monthly site visits, he joined our morning housekeeping huddle just as I was sharing a story. I'd recog-nized a team member who went out of her way to replace a guest's favorite snack – something we encouraged staff to do: notice the little things and go the extra mile. The team cheered. It was a small moment of pride and momentum.

But as soon as the meeting ended, he shook his head and said, "*You're letting the inmates run the asylum.*"

That stuck with me – not because it was clever (it wasn't), but because it revealed exactly how he saw people. To him, employees were replaceable. Tools. Obstacles, even. His version of leadership was fear-based, command-and-control, devoid of empathy or trust.

I stayed in that job longer than I probably should have. I tried to protect the team from his influence as much as I could. But eventually, I got fired. And as hard as that moment was, I felt something unexpected.

Relief.

Because I knew I'd never lead that way. I never wanted anyone to associate my leadership with anxiety, dread, or shame. And while I wouldn't wish that experience on anyone, it taught me more about what kind of leader I wanted to be than any seminar or training ever could.

Now, let me tell you about the best.

Years later, I was working in a corporate leadership role when I got a call that my father - my hero and role model – had been rushed to the ICU. At the time, I was in the middle of a major organizational rollout. Twelve webinars scheduled. Countless hours of prep. The kind of thing most bosses would want you to stay put for.

But when I told my leader what was happening, she didn't hesitate. "Go," she said. "There's nothing more important than being with your dad. We'll figure the rest out."

And I did go. I stayed in the hospital and held my dad's hand every day for 22 days until he passed. I even hosted those webinars from a quiet room the hospital staff let me use. The rollout happened. The company didn't fall apart. And I got to be there for one of the most sacred moments of my life.

I still tell that story, not just because it meant so much to me, but because it was a masterclass in servant leadership. My boss led with empathy. With trust. With humanity. And I would have followed her anywhere.

These two experiences – one that crushed my spirit, and one that restored it – became the foundation for everything this book is about.

Because leadership isn't neutral. It's never neutral.

Every decision you make, every word you speak, every moment you pause (or don't) sends a message to the people you lead. And whether that message builds people up or breaks them down depends entirely on what you believe about their worth.

Do you see them as valuable? Or replaceable?

As humans? Or as tools?

This book is about choosing to see people as _priceless_ – and leading like it matters.

It's about understanding how your actions shape people's thoughts, their feelings, their behavior, and ultimately, their performance.

It's about what happens when leadership becomes less about control and more about care.

So, I'll ask you the same question I've asked hundreds of leaders: _Who was your best leader? Who was your worst? Why?_

Hold those stories close. We're going to come back to them.

And by the end of this journey, I hope you'll not only _know_ the difference between bad and great leadership...you'll _be_ the difference.

But knowing the difference isn't enough — especially when the culture around us rewards results over relationships. In the next chapter, we'll look at what happens when performance becomes the only priority... and what it costs.

So, why talk about this now? Why does people-first leadership matter more today than ever before?

Why This Matters Now

There's a reason people say, *"Employees join companies, but they leave managers."* In today's world, leadership isn't just a position — it's a make-or-break factor for engagement, trust, and well-being.

Maybe you're reading this because your organization is trying to turn things around. Maybe the culture feels strained, the surveys are showing burnout, or people are saying, "I like the mission, but I don't feel seen."

Or maybe things are going well — but you want to strengthen what's already working and go even deeper.

Either way, this book is for you.

If your people are asking for a kinder, more human way of leading...

If you have the heart to lead well but need help turning that into consistent habits...

If you're tired of fear-based cultures, shallow slogans, or watching great people quietly disengage...

Priceless! is here to help.

It's not about being soft. It's about being strong enough to lead with compassion, consistency, and courage. The kind of leadership that doesn't just build performance — but builds people.

The good news? The tides are turning. A new generation of lead-ers is rising — leaders who believe that how we treat people is just as important as what we achieve.

So, my friends, this is your invitation to lead in a way that lifts others, leaves a mark, and reminds people what it feels like to matter. If you're ready to lead differently, it starts here. With one belief: *people are priceless.*

Chapter 1 Wrap-Up: The Value of One

Key Takeaways

- Every person is born with priceless worth regardless of title, performance, or background.

- Leadership is influence, and your influence either affirms or erodes someone's self-worth.

- When you see people as priceless, it changes how you lead, speak, and serve.

- Culture is shaped by the stories people tell about how they were treated.

- You can't truly lead others until you recognize their value and your own.

Reflection Questions

1. Who was the first leader that made you feel truly seen and valued? What did they do?

2. Where might you be unintentionally reinforcing performance-based worth in your team or culture?

3. What would change if you led every person as if their worth was already established?

Mini-Challenge

This week, intentionally affirm someone's worth – especially someone who may not expect it. Look them in the eye and name a strength, character trait, or contribution they bring to the team.

◈ The Priceless Punchline

Q: Why did the scarecrow become a great leader?

A: Because he was outstanding in his field.

Notes (Use this space to capture your thoughts, reactions, or action steps from this chapter)

_____
_____
_____
_____
_____
_____
_____
_____
_____
_____
_____
_____
_____
_____
_____
_____
_____
_____
_____
_____

"You may never know what results come from your actions. But if you do nothing, there will be no result."
— Mahatma Gandhi

The Cost of Performance-First Leadership
*How metrics-first leadership damages
self-worth and culture.*

"What gets measured gets done." It's a phrase often treated like gospel in leadership circles – and it's not wrong. But it's dangerously incomplete. Because what we measure becomes what we value. And what we value becomes how we lead.

When all we measure is performance, that's all we get: performance. Not loyalty. Not trust. Not creativity or compassion or growth. Just numbers. And if those numbers become the only thing we celebrate or scold, we risk turning people into tools.

In today's workplace, the pressure to deliver results has never been higher. Markets are volatile. AI is transforming how we work (and whether some jobs even exist). Customer expectations are changing faster than we can adapt. On top of that, mental health is becoming one of the most pressing issues in the workforce today.

According to a 2024 survey from the American Psychological Association, 92% of workers say it's important for employers to support mental health, but only 38% feel their workplace is doing a good job at it. Stress, uncertainty, and burnout are at all-time highs. And when companies fixate solely on performance metrics in this environment, they're unintentionally making everything worse.

I'm not saying performance doesn't matter. Of course it does. Results matter. Outcomes matter. Businesses need to thrive. But how we get there – that's what defines leadership.

Let me take you back to a culture shift I'll never forget.

I was working for a hospitality brand in the early 2000s. We had a balanced scorecard approach: Guest Satisfaction, Employee Satisfaction, and Financial Results – each weighed equally. The philosophy was simple but strong: take care of your team, and they'll take care of the guest, and the money will follow.

But then came a shift.

A new Senior Vice President of Operations stepped in. The first thing he dismantled? The balance. In his words, "Fluff doesn't drive profit." What he meant by "fluff" was service training, recognition programs, team building, development plans – basically, anything human.

He created a new bonus structure that hinged entirely on a financial audit. Pass the audit, and you unlock the rest of your bonus. Fail it, and you get nothing. Fail twice, and you're fired. No training, no coaching, no support – just an expectation of results.

Our first "practice" audit came back with a score of 38. We scrambled. The next six months were spent in a pressure cooker of spreadsheets, policies, and panic. Guest service took a back seat. Employee morale plummeted. Team meetings turned into audit prep sessions. It was like a hospital obsessed with paperwork while patients flatlined in the waiting room.

What had been a culture of fun, family, and service suddenly became serious, silent, and stressed.

And eventually, I left.

So did many of the other General Managers who had once been fiercely loyal to the brand. We weren't afraid of performance – we were afraid of what it cost when it became the only thing that mattered.

That story's not unique. It happens every day in organizations that confuse compliance with commitment. You can't audit your way into engagement. You can't punish your way into excellence.

Leadership isn't about squeezing more out of people. It's about drawing out the best in them.

John D. Rockefeller – arguably one of the most successful businessmen in history – once said, "*I would pay more for the ability to deal with people than any other ability under the sun.*" That wasn't fluff. That was wisdom. Rockefeller could afford the best technology, the best resources, the best minds. And he knew that none of it mattered if leaders couldn't connect with people.[4]

And I am not the only one. Here's a firsthand account that shows how it feels when performance eclipses people.

What Were They Thinking?
"The System That Broke Us" by Melissa R.

It started out great. I was excited about the job, and the company talked a big game about their culture and values during orientation. But within a few weeks, I realized none of that translated into how we were actually managed.

The moment quarterly numbers came in below target, everything changed. Our director started holding 7 a.m. "accountability calls" every single day, where we were expected to explain what we did yesterday and what we'd do today to hit our targets.

It didn't matter if you were sick or had a death in the family – you showed up, or risked being called out in front of everyone.

One particular morning was especially bad. No one had hit their targets the day before. The director logged onto the call, snapped, and screamed, *"No one is taking this seriously... We're all going to get fired!"*

And then he just slammed his laptop shut.

Reflection Questions:

1. What was Melissa thinking at this moment?

2. How did this affect Melissa's feelings and emotions?

3. What impact did this have on Melissa's behavior and performance?

(Turn to page 151 to read Melissa's real reflections.)

Two Cultures. Two Outcomes. One Choice.

The story you just read isn't rare. It's the natural result of a performance-first culture – a system where metrics matter more than people, and pressure outweighs purpose. But there's another way. People-first cultures don't ignore results – they achieve them differently.

Here's the truth, side by side. One path leads to pressure, fear, and burnout. The other leads to dignity, trust, and growth.

In a performance-first culture:

- Employees are seen as tools to hit numbers.

- Motivation relies on pressure and fear.

- Feedback is top-down and corrective.

- Mistakes are punished.
- Recognition is rare and transactional.
- Success is measured in short-term gains.

The result? A culture of stress, turnover, and silent disengagement.

In a people-first (Priceless) culture:

- Employees are seen as priceless individuals with purpose.
- Motivation is fueled by trust and purpose.
- Feedback is continuous and developmental.
- Mistakes become moments for growth.
- Recognition is frequent, personal, and values-driven.
- Success includes both results and relationships.

The result? A culture of energy, loyalty, and innovation.

As we'll explore in the *Priceless Leadership Model*, leadership behaviors don't exist in a vacuum. Every policy, every comment, every meeting format influences what your people think – which shapes what they feel – which drives how they perform.

And here's the good news: most leaders don't get this wrong because they're heartless. They get it wrong because they're under pressure too – pressure to perform, to prove value, to deliver results. In that pressure, it's easy to start measuring the wrong things.

That's why we need a better lens.

Not to eliminate metrics – but to enrich them with humanity. Because if your dashboard only tracks sales and profits but never trust, retention, or engagement... you're flying blind.

Yes, performance matters. But people matter more.

Because when you take care of your people, performance takes care of itself. Let's stop using carrots and sticks. Let's start using care and strategy.

And if you've been taught that recognition, coaching, and compassion are "fluff"... just wait until you see the results of doing them well.

People-first leadership isn't soft. It's smart. It's strategic. And it's the only kind that builds something that lasts.

So let's stop asking, "How do we squeeze more?" And start asking, "How do we serve better?" Because when you lead with heart, you don't just drive results – you build trust, loyalty, and lives that flourish.

And here's the key: your leadership isn't just shaping performance – it's shaping how people see themselves.

In the next chapter, we'll explore that invisible power – the influence leaders have on thoughts, emotions, and behavior through something deeper: a person's sense of worth.

Chapter 2 Wrap-Up: The System that Broke Us

Key Takeaways

- Performance-first cultures often harm the very people they rely on.

- Leaders shape how people see themselves through everyday choices and behaviors.

- Culture is created by what we consistently celebrate, tolerate, and ignore.

- Seeing people as priceless changes how we design systems and policies.

- Short-term wins aren't worth long-term damage to people's dignity.

Reflection Questions

1. Where have you seen performance valued over people in your workplace?

2. How has that approach affected motivation, morale, and retention?

3. What's one policy, meeting, or metric you could revise to reflect a people-first culture?

Mini-Challenge

This week, pay attention to how success is defined on your team. Is it only numbers, or do people matter too? Before your next team meeting, pause and ask: *"What will this communicate about what we value?"* Then take one intentional step to show that people matter more than performance.

⬧ The Priceless Punchline

Q: Why did the KPI go to therapy?

A: It felt like it never measured up.

Notes (*Use this space to capture your thoughts, reactions, or action steps from this chapter*)

_____
_____
_____
_____
_____
_____
_____
_____
_____
_____
_____
_____
_____
_____
_____
_____
_____
_____
_____
_____

"People don't care how much you know until they know how much you care." – *Theodore Roosevelt*[5]

The Priceless Leadership Model

Understanding the invisible influence leaders have on thoughts, feelings, and performance.

What if the greatest leadership tool isn't strategy or skill... but how you see people?

It's not just a philosophical question. It's the heart of what makes leadership either soar or sink. As leaders, we shape more than behavior – we shape belief. And in this chapter, we'll unpack the Priceless Leadership Model – a practical tool for understanding how leaders can either uplift or unintentionally diminish the people they lead.

Spoiler alert: it's built on one big idea – *every person is priceless!*

The Model That Changed Everything

Of all the tools I've used throughout my career, this one has had the greatest impact – on me, on the people I've led, and on the leaders I've coached. It's simple. It's powerful. And once you understand it, you'll start to see every interaction through a new lens. Let's walk through it together. The model looks like this:

The Priceless Leadership Model: How Worth Shapes Behavior

The Priceless Leadership Model

The diagram shows a cycle that starts with how a person sees themselves (self-image) and flows through thoughts, feelings, and behaviors. At the center of it all is something deeper: their self-worth. This isn't just a psychological model – it's a leadership lens. Because whether leaders realize it or not, their words, tone, habits, and systems influence this cycle every single day. And when you start seeing people through the lens of worth – not just work – you'll begin to understand why they show up the way they do... and how to help them thrive.

This cycle explains why good leadership creates energy – and bad leadership creates anxiety.

Let's break it down.

Self-Image

This is where it starts. Self-image is how we see ourselves in any given moment. And it can change fast. A morning encouragement from a supervisor might lift someone's self-image for the day. A harsh comment in a meeting could tank it.

Webster's defines self-image as: *the idea, conception, or mental image one has of oneself at any point of time.*

When someone's self-image is strong, it fuels positive thoughts. But when it's low? Everything else starts to suffer.

Thoughts

Our thoughts are the stories we tell ourselves. *"I'm capable."* *"I'm falling behind."* *"No one cares what I think."* Those inner narratives grow from our self-image – and leaders influence them more than we realize.

Say a manager rolls their eyes in a meeting. It may seem small, but for the employee presenting, that one moment can spark a flood of self-doubt. Thoughts shift, confidence dips, and the spiral begins.

Feelings

Thoughts shape emotions. When someone thinks, *"I can't do anything right,"* it's only natural they feel defeated, anxious, or sad. Those emotions aren't abstract – they show up in real behaviors at work.

Behaviors

This is the part most managers focus on – because it's what they see. But by the time a behavior shows up (like disengagement, lack of follow-through, or even hostility), it's already been shaped by what's upstream: image, thoughts, and feelings.

Want to change behavior? Start by understanding what's feeding it.

At the heart of it all... *Self-Worth*

Here's the game-changer.

We've been tracing a cycle. But at the center of it all lies something deeper: self-worth. While self-image can change often, self-worth is about the unshakable truth of someone's value. It's who they are – not just what they do.

Webster's defines self-worth as: *a sense of one's own value as a human being.*

And if there's one thing I hope this book helps leaders see, it's this:

Every person you lead is priceless. Not because they're perfect. Not because they hit every target. But because their worth is not determined by performance.

If you embrace that belief, you will lead differently. You'll give feedback with compassion. You'll coach with patience. You'll have hard conversations – but with honor. And your people will respond, because they'll feel seen. Valued. Known.

Real-World Story

Now that we've unpacked the model, let's see what it looks like in action – not in theory, but in a real moment where a leader's response had the power to either crush someone's confidence or restore their worth.

A Positive Disruption

It happened at a large resort during a busy holiday weekend. A front desk employee made a simple mistake with a not-so-simple consequence: he accidentally checked out over 2,000 guests from the system with a single keystroke. Reservations vanished. Lines backed up. Phones started ringing. The panic on his face said it all.

And this is where the story usually goes one of two ways: anger, blame, and shame... or something better.

Kris, the leader on duty, walked over. He didn't yell. He didn't escalate. He calmly handed the employee a bottle of water, pulled him aside, and said, "You're okay. Mistakes happen. We'll figure this out together."

Once the immediate chaos was managed, Kris sat down with him and asked four simple coaching questions:

1. *What happened?*
2. *Why did it happen?*
3. *What did we learn?*
4. *What can we do differently next time?*

That conversation shifted everything. The employee's thoughts began to change – from "I'm an idiot. I'm going to be written up or fired" to *"I'm going to be OK...my leader is so supportive."* His confidence rebounded. His energy returned. He re-engaged.

Kris didn't just fix the mistake. He protected the employee's dignity – and reminded him of his worth. That's what priceless leadership looks like.

The Cycle in Your Life

Kris modeled what it looks like to lead with worth in mind.

Now, take a moment to think about how this cycle has shown up in your own life.

Think back on a time when your self-image was low.

- What were you telling yourself?
- How were you feeling?
- What did it do to your behavior at work?

Now think about a time when you felt on top of the world.

- What were your thoughts then?
- How did those emotions fuel your actions?

Take a moment and jot them down. Then ask yourself:

How do I influence this cycle in others through the way I lead?

And just as great leadership can restore worth, silence and neglect can quietly erode it. Here's one more story that shows how.

What Were They Thinking?

"Invisible" by Chris M.

Six months into my new role, and things *seemed* to be going well. Projects were on track and the team was clicking. I was putting in the hours and doing what I thought was good work.

But my leader was always in his office (or away at some meeting) and did not interact with us very much. I did not get any "thanks" or "here's how you're doing"... not even a passing comment in the hallway.

Then one day, I overheard him praising another team for a big project I had quietly helped bring across the finish line and he didn't even mention me.

Reflection Questions:

1. What was Chris thinking at this moment?
2. How did this affect Chris's feelings and emotions?
3. What impact did this have on Chris's behavior and performance?

(Turn to page 152 to read Chris' real reflections.)

That's the invisible cost of leadership neglect – not cruelty, just absence. Chris didn't need a standing ovation. He needed to be seen. And that's what this model reveals: how easy it is to unintentionally erode someone's worth... and how powerful it is when we do the opposite. But even active leaders can miss the mark when they confuse performance with worth. That brings us to one of the hardest – and most important – mindset shifts a leader must make...

Seeing People Beyond Their Behavior

One of the hardest shifts for any leader is learning to separate a person's behavior from their worth. It's so easy – especially under stress – to reduce someone to what they just said or did.

"He's useless."
"She's a dummy."
"That guy's a jerk."

But people are not their worst moment.

Behavior can be frustrating. Worth stays constant.

When we equate those two (behavior and worth), we dehumanize others. We stop seeing them as individuals with stories, struggles, and potential. We forget their humanity.

This is especially tempting when we don't know someone well – in the workplace, in traffic, on social media. Here's a practice I live and share often:

Pause. Reframe. Humanize.

- That person who just cut you off in traffic? Maybe they're rushing to the hospital.

- That grumpy coworker? Maybe they're carrying grief you can't see.

- That difficult employee? Maybe they've never had a leader who believed in them.

You don't have to excuse the behavior. But you can choose to see the person behind it – and treat them accordingly.

"I don't like what they did or said... but they're still priceless."

It's a simple phrase, but it changes everything – because it keeps us human. It helps us lead from a place of empathy, not ego.

And it reinforces what this whole chapter is about:

How we see people shapes how we treat them.

And how we treat them shapes who they become.

It's not always easy. But it's always worth it. Because when we choose to see people as priceless, we lead in a way that restores rather than reacts.

The Priceless Leadership Model Works

Because when leaders lead through the lens of worth, not just work, everything changes.

As you continue through this book, you'll see how this model connects to all the other themes: feedback, recognition, difficult conversations, trust. But keep this in mind:

> **You cannot call someone to their full potential if you do not first recognize their full worth.**

And that's why this chapter may just be the most important one.

So how do we apply this? If people are influenced by how we treat them, then every moment matters. In the next chapter, we'll explore how everyday leadership habits – the small stuff – can either affirm someone's worth... or erode it.

Chapter 3 Wrap-Up:
The Priceless Leadership Model

Key Takeaways

- Self-worth shapes how people think, feel, and behave – and leaders influence all three, often more than they realize.

- The Priceless Leadership Model helps leaders trace behaviors back to what's really going on beneath the surface.

- Every leader either reinforces or erodes someone's sense of value – there is no neutral ground.

- Focusing only on behavior creates shallow change; addressing self-worth creates lasting transformation.

- You can't call people to greatness if they don't first believe they matter.

Reflection Questions

1. How did your own sense of self-worth grow (or shrink) under past leaders?

2. Where might your leadership be unintentionally weakening someone's self-image or confidence?

3. What's one practical way you can affirm a team member's value this week?

Mini-Challenge

This week, affirm someone for who they are – not just what they do. Compliment their character, their resilience, or their heart. Notice how even a small moment of genuine affirmation can reshape someone's day... or future.

⬦ The Priceless Punchline

Q: Why don't bad leaders believe in gravity?

A: Because they don't understand how their actions carry weight.

Notes (Use this space to capture your thoughts, reactions, or action steps from this chapter)

_____

_____

_____

_____

_____

_____

_____

_____

_____

_____

_____

_____

"Every leadership moment is a mirror — it reflects how we see people, and shapes how they see themselves." – Scott Doggett

Chapter 4:

Priceless in Practice

How everyday actions affirm (or erode) worth – and how to lead with intentional influence.

What we believe about people shapes how we treat them. And how we treat them shapes how they see themselves — and how they show up. That's the quiet power of leadership.

Now that you've seen how thoughts, emotions, and behaviors flow from a person's sense of worth, it's time to turn the lens outward – toward how our leadership choices influence others.

Because when we truly believe people are priceless, it transforms the way we lead: the way we listen, the way we give feedback, the way we respond in hard moments, and the way we create environments where people can thrive.

And what we model in small moments – especially when no one's watching – can either build someone's belief in their worth or quietly break it.

The Power of Influence

You don't need a title to be a leader. You only need someone watching you. And whether you realize it or not, you are constantly influencing the thoughts, emotions, and behaviors of those around you.

Take a moment to consider this: *How many people have you influenced today – intentionally or unintentionally?* A raised eyebrow. A kind word. A long pause. A short reply. Every one of these things sends a message.

If you've made it this far in the book, you now understand how deeply a person's self-image, thoughts, emotions, and behaviors are connected. And you know that those things cycle back into the way someone sees themselves. The question is: *are you a positive part of that cycle?*

What You Do Matters

When you see people as priceless, you begin to realize that your influence isn't just a leadership tool — it's a responsibility.

Here are a few simple but powerful ways leaders affirm the worth of others every day:

- Expressing appreciation, even if just to say, *"I see you. Thank you."*

- Reminding people who they are, not just what they've done.

- Pausing to listen even when your calendar is full.

- Celebrating progress, not just perfection.

- Giving specific feedback about what someone is doing well and how to build on it.

- Offering redirection without shame when someone makes a mistake.

- Being flexible when someone's life circumstances require understanding.

- Helping people grow by asking about their goals and finding ways to support them.

- Making life easier by doing little things that matter — like finishing the schedule well in advance so people can plan their lives.

- Providing the tools, training, and information people need to be successful.

These aren't just best practices – they're signs of someone who understands the true worth of a human being. And in time, these habits shape a culture.

Don't Kill the Goose

One of the most well-known fables is that of *"The Goose and the Golden Egg"*. In it, a farmer discovers that one of his geese lays a golden egg every morning. At first, he is overjoyed. But soon, he becomes greedy. He wants more eggs, faster. So, in a moment of impatience, he kills the goose, thinking he'll find a treasure trove inside. Instead, he finds nothing – and he's lost the one thing that was producing the treasure all along.

It's a funny little story... until you realize how often we do the same thing in leadership. I often share this parable with leaders to illustrate a painful truth: when we focus on results alone, and we forget to nurture the people who produce those results, we eventually lose both.

Of course, leadership missteps aren't always dramatic. Sometimes, the damage is in what's not said. Here's one story of a missed opportunity.

What Were They Thinking?

"The Breaking Point" by Tanya M.

I'm a nurse. I didn't get into this type of work for praise or because it was easy (it's not) — I got into it to care for people. But after two years of being short-staffed, things started to get bad. Nurses and other staff were leaving faster than we could replace them, and leadership just kept saying, "Help is on the way" but it never came.

We had overcrowded hallways with patients, more and more reports and meetings being asked of us, and even a completely new computer system to learn in the middle of all the craziness. I was working 60+ hours a week and was skipping lunch breaks, not even having time some days to go to the bathroom, and often missed dinner at home with the family.

I remember sitting one day in the break room after a difficult patient discharge. I just sat there, staring at the wall for like 10 straight minutes...

Reflection Questions:

1. What was Tanya thinking at this moment?

2. How did this affect Tanya's feelings and emotions?

3. What impact did this have on Tanya's behavior and performance?

(Turn to page 152 to read Tanya's real reflections.)

You don't need to be a nurse to understand this moment. You've likely had your own version – the kind of day where silence feels louder than words. It doesn't always take cruelty to crush someone's spirit. Sometimes, it's just the slow erosion of care – the silence, the inaction, the refusal to see what people are carrying.

But what if things were different?

Imagine a world where leaders chose to affirm worth in every encounter. Where people walked away from meetings feeling more confident than when they walked in. Where teams were built not just on performance metrics, but on mutual respect and trust. Where coaching wasn't just for correction, but a way to call out potential. Where trust wasn't a buzzword on the wall — but a lived experience every day.

What kind of workplaces would we create? What kind of people would we become?

> **When we choose to see others as priceless, it changes how we lead – and it can change the world.**

Before we turn the page to Servant Leadership, pause. Think about the people you lead, work with, or care about. What do they believe about their worth – and how has your leadership shaped that story?

Your influence matters. And now that you see the impact you have, the question becomes:

What kind of leader will you choose to be?

Next Up: Servant Leadership

So how do we lead with greater care, clarity, and purpose? How do we turn the belief that people are priceless into daily habits that reflect it?

In *Part II,* we'll explore the foundation of Servant leadership – its spiritual roots, its business case, and its timeless impact. You'll also encounter a special assessment designed to help you reflect, grow, and create a development plan tailored to your journey.

It all begins with one truth:
People are priceless.
Let's lead like we believe it.

Chapter 4 Wrap-Up: Priceless in Practice

Key Takeaways

- Leadership is influence – and it always shapes someone's story about themselves.

- Everyday moments, not grand gestures, build a culture that values people.

- When leaders overlook the weight their teams are carrying, it's not just inefficient – it's dehumanizing.

- Like the Goose and the Golden Egg, it reminds us: if we chase results and neglect people, we risk losing both.

- You don't have to be perfect to lead well – but you do have to be present, aware, and intentional.

Reflection Questions

1. When was the last time your words or actions left a lasting impact – positive or negative?

2. What story are you writing in the hearts of the people you lead?

3. Where might your team be experiencing silent strain, and how can you respond with empathy and action?

Mini-Challenge

Choose one person on your team. Ask yourself: *"What would it look like to lead this person as if their worth was priceless?"* Then take one action this week that shows them you see, value, and support them.

♦ The Priceless Punchline

Q: What's a leader's favorite type of music?

A: Feedback.

Notes *(Use this space to capture your thoughts, reactions, or action steps from this chapter)*

_____

_____

_____

_____

_____

_____

_____

_____

_____

_____

_____

_____

_____

"People may forget what you said, but they will never forget how you made them feel." – *Maya Angelou* [6]

Part II:

THE WAY OF THE SERVANT LEADER

Now that we've laid the foundation – the heart-level truths about leadership, influence, and worth – it's time to walk the path of the servant leader.

This next section is about choosing a better way. The world often tells us to lead from the front with power, pressure, and performance. But Jesus modeled something radically different: leading through humility, love, and service.

Servant leadership isn't weak. It's not about stepping back – it's about stepping in. It's courageous, countercultural, and transformational. And it works – not just in faith-based organizations, but in any workplace that wants to build trust, inspire excellence, and unlock the full potential of its people.

In the chapters ahead, we'll explore what servant leadership really means, why it matters, and how you can live it out right where you are. You'll also be introduced to the *Priceless Leadership Assessment* – a simple but powerful tool to help you grow in the habits that make servant leaders unforgettable.

Let's go deeper.

"Whoever wants to become great among you must be your servant." — Matthew 20:26 (NIV)

Servant Leadership

What it is...and what it's not.
(Jesus, Greenleaf, and today's workplace)[7]

If leadership is influence, then servant leadership is influence on purpose. After seeing how small actions can affirm someone's worth, this chapter explores the mindset that drives those actions – and why the best leaders start by serving first.

Before servant leadership became a business buzzword, it was a basin and a towel.

Jesus, the Son of God, got on His knees and washed His disciples' feet. It wasn't during a casual lunch. It was the night before the cross – when betrayal, denial, and suffering loomed heavy. And still... He chose to serve. Not to prove a point. Not to stage a metaphor. But to model a way of life.

He didn't just preach humility – He practiced it.

This, I believe, is the original picture of leadership at its best: not a show of power, but an act of service. Not just directing others, but lifting them up. Not a title or a throne, but a towel and a basin.

Servant Leadership Defined

Modern organizations owe a lot to Robert Greenleaf, who coined the term servant leadership in 1970 after reading <u>Journey to the East</u> by Hermann Hesse. Greenleaf, then an AT&T executive, came to believe that the best leaders are first and foremost servants – those whose primary motivation is to support the growth and well-being of their people and communities.[8]

His guiding question was simple but radical:

"Do those served grow as persons?"

If not, the leader wasn't truly leading.

At its core, servant leadership is a mindset and a model that turns traditional power structures upside-down. Instead of seeing people as tools to achieve the leader's goals, the servant leader sees their role as empowering others to thrive and succeed. Their goal is not control, but contribution. Not recognition, but impact. Not ego, but love.

What Servant Leadership Is Not

Let's clear up a few common misconceptions:

- It's not soft. Servant leaders have high expectations. They just deliver them with grace.

- It's not passive. Servant leaders act decisively and make decisions with others in mind.

- It's not about pleasing everyone. They aim to do what's right, not what's popular.

- It's not *"inmates running the asylum."* It's leaders choosing to dignify, not dominate.

- It's not avoiding hard conversations – it's about doing it in a way that uplifts instead of tears down.

- It doesn't mean ignoring performance – it means knowing that performance without people is hollow.

Why Servant Leadership Matters Now

We live in a world that is anxious, distracted, and burned out.

Between economic uncertainty, AI-driven disruption, political division, and mental health struggles, employees are showing up with invisible burdens. And yet many leaders still operate like they're managing machines instead of human beings.

They demand more, while offering less.

They celebrate hustle, but neglect health.

They push for innovation, while starving people of inspiration.

That's why servant leadership is more relevant now than ever before.

It's not just a feel-good idea – it's the most human, effective, and sustainable way to lead. Servant leaders create spaces where people can breathe, belong, and become. And when people feel valued, they give their best – not out of fear, but out of pride and purpose.

The Business Case: A Quick Preview

Don't worry – we'll get to the hard data in an upcoming chapter. But here's a preview of the case we'll make:

- Companies like Southwest Airlines, Chick-fil-A, 3M and many other well-known brands have been consistently praised for creating servant-led cultures that prioritize people and perform at a high level.[9]

- The Harvard Service-Profit Chain backs this up: happy, supported employees create better customer experiences, which leads to loyalty, growth, and results.[10]

So you see... servant leadership isn't just moral – it's strategic.

What It Looks Like in Action

Servant leadership isn't just a moral ideal – it's a practical, people-centered strategy that creates environments where everyone can thrive, not just survive. And that's especially true for people who are often overlooked.

In far too many workplaces, employees from marginalized backgrounds – whether due to race, gender, ability, age, or socioeconomic status – feel invisible. Their voices go unheard. Their contributions get overlooked. Their potential is underestimated.

Servant leadership offers a different path. It doesn't ignore differences – it honors them. And it makes space for everyone to belong, contribute, and lead.

It prioritizes dignity over dominance. It sees every team member as a person to serve, not a resource to manage. And in doing so, it creates cultures where people of all backgrounds can contribute fully, grow authentically, and lead boldly.

So what does this look like in real life? What happens when a company doesn't just talk about servant leadership, but builds its entire culture around it?

Meet TDIndustries – a company that doesn't just use servant leadership language but lives it out daily, from the front lines to the executive team.[11]

Case Study:
TDIndustries – Servant Leadership in Action [12]

Founded in 1946, TDIndustries (TD) is not only one of the leading mechanical construction and facility services companies in the U.S., but also a gold standard in servant leadership. TD's CEO and executive team have long embraced Robert Greenleaf's principles, embedding them into the very structure and soul of the company.[13]

At TD, leadership isn't about hierarchy – it's about responsibility. The company refers to its leaders as "servant leaders," and that mindset shapes every facet of their culture. Leaders are evaluated not only on performance metrics, but on how well they grow, support, and develop others – especially those who may have been overlooked in traditional leadership pipelines. It's a model that values people for who they are, not just what they produce.

Employees are encouraged to give 360-degree feedback to their managers, creating a culture of transparency, psychological safety, and mutual respect. And leadership development isn't reserved for executives – it's nurtured at every level, helping create opportunity for people from all backgrounds to grow and thrive.

One of the most distinctive practices at TD is the consistent use of "voice of the employee" surveys and pulse checks. These tools aren't just checkboxes – they inform decision-making, team structure, development pathways, and wellness initiatives. In other words, TD listens deeply – and acts on what they hear.

TD is also 100% employee-owned, giving every employee a true stake in the company's success. That ownership model reinforces a culture of mutual care and shared responsibility – where dignity, equity, and excellence go hand-in-hand.

The results speak for themselves: TDIndustries has been featured on Fortune's "100 Best Companies to Work For" list more than 20 times. Their low turnover, high engagement, and continued profitability prove that servant leadership isn't just a philosophy – it's a competitive advantage rooted in human flourishing.[14]

How This Connects to You

Servant leadership starts in your spirit and shows up in your habits.

It's not about being perfect – it's about being present.

It's not about charisma – it's about consistency.

As we move into the next chapters, we'll look at the core habits and traits of servant leaders, assess how we're doing, and develop a personalized growth plan.

But first, here's your moment of reflection...

Imagine...

Imagine if every team meeting started with the question, *"How can I serve you today?"*

Imagine if every leader saw themselves as stewards, not bosses.

Imagine a world where every person you lead walks away with a deeper sense of dignity, purpose, and possibility.

That's the world we're building. And you're the kind of leader who can build it.

What's Next

So, what does a servant leader actually *do?*

What traits define this way of leading?

And how can you grow those traits in yourself – and call them out in others?

That's what we'll unpack in the next few chapters.

We'll begin with a short reflection tool – *the Priceless Leadership Assessment* – to help you identify where you're strong, where you might be stuck, and where God might be calling you to grow.

Then, we'll walk through the twelve core traits of servant leadership – grouped into 3 categories *(Heart, Head, and Hands)* – and guide you in building a development plan that fits your unique journey.

Chapter 5 Wrap-Up:
The Way of the Servant Leader

Key Takeaways

- Servant leadership flips the script: it's not about being in charge – it's about caring for those in your charge.

- Jesus modeled servant leadership not as a strategy, but as a way of being.

- Robert Greenleaf helped bring the concept into modern leadership conversations, but the roots go back much further.[15]

- Servant leaders prioritize people over power, presence over position, and purpose over profit.

- Leading this way is not soft – it requires strength, courage, and humility

Reflection Questions

1. In what ways do you already reflect servant leadership? Where is it hardest?

2. How does your current leadership style align – or clash – with Jesus' example?

3. What are the myths about servant leadership you need to unlearn?

Mini-Challenge

This week, choose one task you'd normally delegate or overlook. Then jump in – not to prove a point, but to shoulder the load. Let your presence speak louder than your position.

🔷 The Priceless Punchline

Q: Why did the servant leader refuse the corner office?
A: Because they preferred being in everyone else's corner.

Notes *(Use this space to capture your thoughts, reactions, or action steps from this chapter)*

_____

_____

_____

_____

_____

_____

_____

_____

_____

_____

_____

_____

_____

_____

_____

_____

"The true leader is a servant first." – *Robert Greenleaf*[16]

Chapter 6:

How Do You Lead

*A self-assessment to discover where your servant leadership shines –
and where it can grow.*

*Knowing you want to lead like a servant is one thing – knowing how
you're wired to serve is another.*

Before you can grow in servant leadership, you need to understand the strengths and struggles that shape your influence.
That's where this next section comes in.

You've seen the vision. You've read the stories. You've felt the
pull of a different kind of leadership – one rooted in worth, not
ego. Now, it's time to hold up the mirror.

How are you really doing as a servant leader?

This chapter introduces the *Priceless Leadership Self-Assessment*
– a simple tool designed to help you reflect on how well your
leadership aligns with the values we've been exploring. This
isn't about guilt or perfection. It's about awareness. It's about
noticing where you shine, and where there's room to grow.

But before we jump into scoring yourself, let's acknowledge
something important:

What Gets in the Way? (And What Gets You Through)

Servant leadership sounds great in theory. But in real life? It can
feel risky, messy, and even countercultural. If you've ever
struggled to lead this way consistently, you're not alone.

Here are some common roadblocks — and some truths that can help you push through:

Obstacle	The Truth
Fear of Appearing Weak	Servant leadership isn't soft — it's strong. It takes real courage to apologize, listen, and elevate others.
Pressure from Upper Leadership	You may not control the culture above you — but you can influence the culture around you. Change often starts with one person.
Lack of Time or Structure	You don't need hours of extra time to lead this way. A moment of care, clarity, or presence goes further than you think.
Toxic Past Role Models	If you've only seen fear-based leadership, it's easy to default to what you know. But you can break the cycle.
Burnout or Compassion Fatigue	You can't serve well if your soul is running on empty. Rest isn't selfish — it's strategic. Refill the cup. Reset the heart.

Let's Reflect Before We Score

If any of those roadblocks hit a little close to home, you're not alone. Every leader carries some tension — between how they want to lead and how they actually show up. That doesn't mean you're failing. It means you're human.

This next step is about awareness, not achievement. It's a mirror, not a grade. You're simply pausing to notice where your heart, head, and hands are strongest — and where you may be invited to grow. So take a breath. Be honest. Be kind to yourself. And most of all — be curious. That's where real growth begins.

How to Take the Assessment

You'll rate yourself across 12 traits of servant leadership — grouped into three domains: Heart, Head, and Hands. Each one includes a brief description to guide your reflection.

Don't worry about overthinking it or getting the "right" answer. There's no trophy at the end — just insight. Go with your gut and be as real as you can.

Once you've scored each trait, total the numbers in each domain. Your highest domain will point to your current leadership strength. The pattern of your scores will help identify your leadership style profile — a helpful snapshot of how you tend to lead today.

You'll use these insights again in *Chapter 9* when we create your personal leadership development plan. So keep your scores close — they're going to keep helping you grow.

Ready? Let's take an honest look at how you lead — and where your greatest growth might be waiting.

The Priceless Leadership Assessment

Instructions:

Rate yourself for each of the 12 traits below using this scale:

1 = **Rarely true of me**
2 = **Sometimes true**
3 = **Often true**
4 = **Consistently true**
5 = **A defining part of who I am as a leader**

Trait	Description	Score (1–5)
Empathy	I take time to understand others' perspectives and feelings.	_____
Humility	I admit mistakes, ask for feedback, and give others credit.	_____
Integrity	I do what's right, even when no one's watching.	_____
Compassion	I respond to others with care, patience, and kindness.	_____
Vision	I inspire others with a clear, meaningful direction.	_____
Wisdom	I apply discernment to tough choices and complex situations.	_____
Accountability	I hold myself and others responsible for commitments and behavior.	_____
Discernment	I pause to pray, reflect, and seek insight before acting or advising.	_____

Trait	Description	Score (1–5)
Service	I look for ways to support others – especially behind the scenes.	_____
Empowerment	I equip and trust others to take ownership and grow.	_____
Stewardship	I manage time, resources, and influence in ways that honor others.	_____
Courage	I speak the truth in love and make hard decisions with care.	_____

Add up your scores for each domain below to discover your unique leadership profile:

- **Heart** (Empathy, Humility, Integrity, Compassion): _____
- **Head** (Vision, Wisdom, Accountability, Discernment): _____
- **Hands** (Service, Empowerment, Stewardship, Courage): _____

Leadership Style Profiles

Discovering Your Servant Leadership Archetype

Your scores aren't just numbers – they're clues. They point to patterns, priorities, and potential. Each domain *(Heart, Head, and Hands)* plays a vital role in servant leadership. The way your scores cluster can highlight your current strengths and where your next stretch may be.

The seven profiles below represent common leadership patterns. They're not boxes to squeeze into – they're mirrors. Let them reflect where you are now and reveal what's possible next.

Each includes an example of a biblical and modern-day leader who modeled this style – not to compare, but to inspire.

How to Find Your Profile

Look at your total scores in each domain:

- **High score** = Your highest-scoring domain
- **Low score** = The domain(s) that score at least 2 points lower than your highest
- **Equal or similar scores** (within 1 point) = Considered "balanced"

Then, identify your pattern using the 7 profiles below – each one designed to help you grow with purpose.

---

1. The Guardian

Score pattern: High Heart, lower Head and Hands
Snapshot: You lead with deep care, integrity, and emotional intelligence. People feel seen and safe with you – a true gift.
Challenge: You may struggle with strategy, follow-through, or difficult conversations.
Growth invitation: Strengthen your clarity, structure, and courageous accountability.
Next step: Practice pairing warmth with wisdom – like giving direct feedback with compassion.
Modern Example: Fred Rogers (Mr. Rogers) – brought deep emotional presence and values-based messaging to children's TV.
Biblical Example: John the Baptist – modeled humility, conviction, and purposeful preparation for others.

2. The Strategist

Score pattern: High Head, lower Heart and Hands
Snapshot: You lead with insight, logic, and long-term thinking. Others look to you for direction.
Challenge: You may come off as detached or overly task-driven.
Growth invitation: Slow down and connect more personally with your team.
Next step: Schedule weekly check-ins or mentoring moments to build relational depth.
Modern Example: Angela Merkel – led Germany with steady wisdom through complex global challenges.
Biblical Example: Solomon – asked God for wisdom and ruled with discernment (though not without flaws).

3. The Doer

Score pattern: High Hands, lower Heart and Head
Snapshot: You are reliable, selfless, and quick to take action. You show love by serving.
Challenge: You may miss the forest for the trees, staying so busy you lose sight of purpose or people.
Growth invitation: Step back and reflect on what really matters.
Next step: Block time weekly to realign with your vision and values.
Modern Example: Mother Teresa – met physical needs with relentless service while inspiring deeper compassion.
Biblical Example: Ruth – faithfully served Naomi, trusting God with the bigger picture.

4. The Architect

Score pattern: High Head and Hands, lower Heart
Snapshot: You combine strategic thinking with strong execution – a natural builder and problem-solver.
Challenge: You may overlook emotional needs or relational tension in the team.
Growth invitation: Deepen empathy and presence in your daily leadership.
Next step: Pause in meetings to ask how people are feeling – not just what they're doing.
Modern Example: Tim Cook – guided Apple's operations and vision while learning to show more personal leadership.
Biblical Example: Moses (early years) – focused on logistics and delegation, later grew into deeper compassion.

5. The Bridgebuilder

Score pattern: High Heart and Head, lower Hands
Snapshot: You inspire with care and clarity. People trust your motives and your message.
Challenge: You may hesitate to take action or fully empower others.
Growth invitation: Translate your good intentions into consistent leadership practices.
Next step: Delegate boldly, coach others, and turn vision into momentum.
Modern Example: Barack Obama – often paired inspiration and intellect, yet faced critique over execution gaps.
Biblical Example: Paul – wrote with passion and precision, while growing in relational and practical leadership.

6. The Champion

Score pattern: High Heart and Hands, lower Head
Snapshot: You love well and serve hard. You lift others up with humility and action.
Challenge: You may lack long-term vision or structure, leading to burnout or misalignment.
Growth invitation: Build strategic thinking and discernment into your leadership rhythm.
Next step: Spend time monthly on goal setting, prayerful reflection, and learning.
Modern Example: Howard Schultz (Starbucks) – emphasized people-first values and service, with a learning curve in long-term strategy.
Biblical Example: Barnabas – empowered others with generosity and care; mentored Paul but deferred strategy.

7. The Integrator

Score pattern: Balanced across Heart, Head, and Hands (all within 1 point)

Snapshot: You're steady and holistic – emotionally present, strategically minded, and action-driven.

Challenge: You might coast on competency or miss a deeper area of growth.

Growth invitation: Don't settle for balance – sharpen it. Keep growing into your next season.

Next step: Choose one trait in each domain to develop intentionally in the next 90 days.

Modern Example: Dr. Martin Luther King Jr. – led with vision, compassion, and bold action.

Biblical Example: Nehemiah – integrated prayer, planning, and servant execution to rebuild a nation.

Final Word

This assessment isn't a label. It's a lens.

It helps you see your leadership more clearly – not just where you stand, but where you're headed. Every number you circled reflects a real-life behavior that's shaping your team's culture, performance, and sense of worth.

This moment of reflection is a starting point, not a finish line.

You don't have to be perfect to be powerful. You just have to be willing – to learn, to stretch, to lead differently.

Because leadership isn't about having all the answers.
It's about asking the right questions.
And the best one might be:

What kind of legacy am I leaving in the hearts of those I lead?

Keep that question close.
Let it guide your next conversation, your next decision, your next step.

The path of the servant leader begins right where you are – and it starts again every day.

Let the mirror become a map.

Let's keep walking it together.

What's Next

In the coming chapters, we'll unpack each of the three domains (Heart, Head, and Hands) and walk through the twelve core traits of servant leadership.

You'll find practical tools, real stories, and tangible insights to help you grow in the areas that matter most.

Keep your scores nearby – you'll come back to them when we build your personalized development plan in Chapter 9.

Chapter 6 Wrap-Up: How Do You Lead?

Key Takeaways

- Every leader leaves a legacy – whether intentional or accidental.

- Your leadership behaviors shape how others feel, perform, and see themselves.

- The Priceless Leadership Assessment helps you reflect on who you are, not just what you do.

- Great leaders grow from the inside out – starting with the heart, then the head, then the hands.

- Awareness is the first step to transformation. You can't grow what you're not willing to see.

- The way your traits cluster tells a story — one that's worth paying attention to.

Reflection Questions

1. Which traits from the assessment are your strongest? Which need growth?

2. How do your behaviors currently affect the self-worth of those you lead?

3. What leadership habits are forming your reputation and legacy?

4. Which profile felt most like you — and what will you do with that insight?

Mini-Challenge

Ask three trusted people (a peer, a direct report, and a friend) to share one strength and one opportunity they see in your leadership. Listen with humility – then take one step toward growth.

♦ The Priceless Punchline

Q: Why did the leader bring a selfie stick to the workshop?
A: Because they heard it was time to take a long, hard look at themselves.

Notes (Use this space to capture your thoughts, reactions, or action steps from this chapter)

_____

_____

_____

_____

_____

_____

_____

_____

_____

_____

_____

"The growth and development of people is the highest calling of leadership." – Harvey S. Firestone

Chapter 7:

Scaling Servant Leadership
How Heart, Head, and Hands Evolve with Leadership Scope

Servant Leadership: A Calling at Every Level

Titles change. Calendars fill. Responsibilities grow. But your calling stays the same: *serve first*. But as your influence grows, so does your impact – and your responsibility.

Your circle gets bigger. The ripple gets wider. And the way you serve must stretch with it.

Just like a tree's branches stretch wider as it grows, your leadership must expand to reach farther while staying rooted in the same soil: Heart, Head, and Hands.

This chapter explores how servant leadership evolves as your influence grows — across three key levels of leadership:

1. Leading Others
2. Leading Teams or Departments
3. Leading Organizations

Each level brings new challenges, new opportunities, and new expressions of the same servant leadership DNA. Whether your profile was the Guardian, Champion, Strategist — or one of the other powerful combinations — this next step is about putting those strengths into action at the right level. Because great leaders don't just grow personally — they help others grow, too.

The Evolution of Heart, Head, and Hands

Let's take a closer look at how the core traits of servant leadership evolve as your scope expands.

---

1. Leading Others: The Frontline

Frontline leaders are the heartbeat of the organization. They're in the trenches — giving feedback, answering questions, calming storms, and celebrating wins. Their leadership shapes the daily experience of employees more than any memo from the C-suite.

At this level, servant leadership looks like:

- **Heart**: Knowing your people. Listening well. Celebrating often.
  Ask yourself: How am I showing care and building trust daily?

- **Head**: Solving real-time problems and providing crystal-clear expectations.
  What problems need solving right now?

- **Hands**: Giving feedback, providing tools, coaching performance, and being visibly present.
  How can I support performance today in tangible ways?

I once heard an Executive say...

"The higher you go up in an organization, the less important you are to the day-to-day. If a frontline leader disappears for a week, the team feels it immediately."

If you're leading from the frontlines, don't underestimate your impact. You're not just managing people — you're shaping their stories.

2. Leading Teams: The Department Level

Now you're leading leaders. Your focus shifts from managing tasks to multiplying impact. You're not just solving problems — you're equipping others to solve them well.

At this level, servant leadership looks like:

- **Heart**: Coaching and developing your managers. Knowing their strengths and struggles.
  Ask yourself: How am I developing and championing my leaders?

- **Head**: Translating strategy into priorities. Navigating cross-functional complexity.
  Are we aligned with our mission and with one another?

- **Hands**: Removing roadblocks. Building trust between teams. Budgeting for what matters — development, wellness, and recognition.
  What's getting in their way — and how can I remove it?

Your leadership isn't just personal anymore — it's contagious. Are the leaders beneath you learning to serve, or simply to survive? Your presence sets the tone. The culture you create for your leaders is the culture they'll create for their teams.

---

3. Leading Organizations: The Executive Level

Here, servant leadership either multiplies the mission or sabotages it. You set the tone, pace, and policies that shape how leadership is experienced across the board.

At this level, servant leadership looks like:

- **Heart**: Prioritizing people in your decisions — even when it's inconvenient.

    Ask yourself: Are people centered in the policies and choices I make?

- **Head**: Balancing vision with systems thinking. *Are we designing systems that support both our mission and the people behind it?*

- **Hands**: Modeling visibility, humility, and care. Walking the halls. Hosting open forums. Being human. *Am I visible, present, and modeling what truly matters?*

At this level, presence is everything. Not just your strategy — your humanity. Leadership at this level isn't about being the loudest voice — it's about listening to the quietest ones.

Same Heart. Wider Reach.

The traits don't change — but the scale does. Here's a quick snapshot of how the Heart, Head, and Hands of a servant leader evolve as your influence grows:

	Heart (Who You Are)	Head (How You Think)	Hands (What You Do)
Leading Others	Show care, build trust, celebrate individuals	Solve problems, set direction	Give feedback, coach, provide tools
Leading Teams	Develop leaders, champion growth	Align goals, manage complexity	Remove barriers, foster collaboration
Leading Organizations	Lead with compassion, shape culture through policy	Cast vision, steward systems	Model visibility, steward influence and resources

As you grow, servant leadership must grow with you. And just like we saw in Chapter 6, each leadership style profile has unique strengths — but those strengths must scale:

- A *Guardian* at the executive level must grow bolder.

- A *Strategist* leading a team must grow warmer.

- A *Champion* moving up must grow wiser.

- An *Integrator* in the middle must grow clearer.

Let your growth match your reach.

As your leadership scope expands, your style must stretch with it. The strengths that served you well in one season may need refining in the next. Servant leaders don't outgrow their core —

they deepen it, adapting with humility, courage, and wisdom. That's the real growth journey.

But here's the deeper shift: as your influence grows, so does your responsibility. Not just to do more — but to serve more. And that brings us back to a powerful visual that flips traditional leadership thinking on its head.

The Pyramid Flip (Revisited)

Remember the inverted leadership pyramid from Chapter 5? Let's look at it again — through the lens of everything we've just discussed:

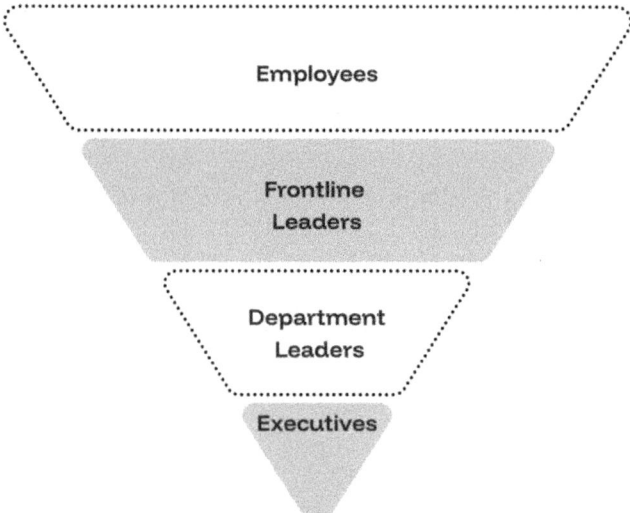

Why flip the pyramid? Because in servant leadership, the higher your title, the deeper your responsibility. The more influence you have, the more people you're called to serve.

This is the paradox — and the power — of servant leadership:

You don't rise to the top to be served. You descend into greatness by lifting others.

True leadership doesn't sit on top — it carries the weight of the culture. It creates space. It sets tone. It serves.

As your leadership grows, don't just ask, 'What can I control?' Ask, 'Who can I support?' That's the question that flips the pyramid — and multiplies your impact.

Warning: Traps at Every Level (and How to Dodge Them)

The pyramid may be flipped, but gravity still applies — and the weight gets heavier as you go down. Each level carries unique burdens and blind spots that can quietly derail your impact if you're not paying attention. Awareness is your first line of defense. Rhythms of reflection and support are your second.

So before we move on, let's pause and name those traps — and offer some wisdom to help you navigate them.

Frontline Leaders

Common Traps:

- Drowning in daily crises
- Becoming the team's fixer instead of its coach
- Prioritizing productivity over people
- Feeling unsupported, untrained, or isolated

How to Dodge Them:

- *Don't carry it alone* — create peer support or lean on a mentor.

- *Coach, don't rescue.* Instead of fixing everything yourself, help others solve problems.

- *Celebrate small wins* — morale lives in the daily moments.

- *Create healthy boundaries* to prevent burnout (and model them for your team).

- *Ask for help* — it's not weakness, it's wisdom.

Pro Tip: Spend 10 minutes each day walking around and checking in — not with an agenda, but with curiosity.

Mid-Level Leaders

Common Traps:

- Feeling stuck in the middle — pressure from above, problems from below

- Losing your identity in execution

- Emotional fatigue from managing both up and down

- Drifting from direct connection with people

How to Dodge Them:

- *Stay rooted in purpose.* Remind yourself why you lead — not just what you lead.

- *Champion your team upward* — advocate for their needs in strategic spaces.

- *Create "shoulder-to-shoulder" time* with your managers. Don't just meet — collaborate.

- *Balance direction with development* — push for results while growing people.

- *Name the tension.* Invite honest conversations across levels.

Pro Tip: Make a monthly rhythm to review both strategy and culture — because if you don't protect the people side, the strategy won't stick.

Executive Leaders

Common Traps:

- Isolation at the top

- Relying on filtered feedback

- Leading from spreadsheets instead of stories

- Losing visibility or emotional connection to staff

- Substituting policies for presence

How to Dodge Them:

- *Walk the halls* (in person or virtually). Ask open-ended questions and listen longer than you speak.

- *Establish unfiltered feedback loops* — peer forums, skip-levels, anonymous staff insights.

- *Use your platform to amplify values* — not just results.

- *Name your blind spots and invite others to speak into them.*

- *Lead with humanity.* Vulnerability at the top gives permission everywhere else.

Pro Tip: Host quarterly listening sessions with no agenda. Just ask: *What's giving you life? What's draining you?* Then take notes — and take action.

Final Wisdom Across All Levels:

- *Build rhythms of reflection* — weekly, monthly, quarterly.

- *Stay curious* — about your team, your own patterns, and what's changing around you.

- *Don't drift alone* — community is a lifeline, not a luxury.

- *Servant leadership is a daily practice*, not a one-time choice.

Sometimes, the drift happens slowly. Other times, it hits us head-on — like being thrown into leadership without a map. That's exactly what happened to David.

David's story is one many leaders know too well. It captures the cost of overlooking leadership support — and why *how* we develop leaders matters just as much as who we promote.

What Were They Thinking?
"Just Get It Done" by David R.

I got promoted to a team lead role at my call center and was assigned three direct reports, but I never really got any additional training, and it was my first leadership job ever. My manager told me to just keep doing what I was doing. He said, "You've got a team now – figure it out." It was like he was testing me or something.

I did my best, but I remember one time I was struggling with one of my agents who was missing his targets and struggling, and I wasn't sure what to do. When I asked my boss, he basically just shrugged and said, "That's why we made you the lead — it's your problem now."

Reflection Questions:

1. What was David thinking in this moment?

2. How did it affect his emotions?

3. What impact did it have on his performance?

(Turn to page 153 to read David's real reflections.)

Moments like these don't just frustrate new leaders – they quietly erode confidence and self-worth. And the ripple doesn't stop there. David's story reminds us: leadership isn't always clear-cut. It's often a stretch between old expectations and new responsibilities. When you're leading from the middle, it's easy to feel pulled in opposite directions.

But tension isn't a sign you're failing. It's a sign you're growing.

Let's explore how to lead well when you find yourself caught between levels.

Leading Between Levels

Most leaders don't live neatly in one box. Titles might say "Manager" or "Director," but real life is messier. One minute, you're rolling up your sleeves with a team member. The next, you're in a strategic planning session trying to shape the future.

Welcome to the tension of the in-between.

You may find yourself pulled between expectations from above and needs from below — stretched like a bridge between two worlds. But that's not a flaw in your leadership. That's the front line of transformation.

When your scope is split:

- *Lead with clarity in each context.* Don't blend the boundaries. Know what each group needs from you — and be present accordingly.

- *Zoom in, then zoom out.* Frontline issues need empathy and urgency. Strategy rooms need calm thinking and big-picture focus.

- *Name the tension.* It's okay to admit to your team, "I'm juggling multiple hats right now — but I'm here for you." Authenticity builds trust.

- *Ask better questions.* "What's the most important thing I can do for you right now?" can break through the noise and build connection fast.

- *Protect your soul.* This space can be exhausting. Build rhythms of renewal — prayer, coaching, reflection, Sabbath. Leadership doesn't flow from burnout; it flows from overflow.

Servant leadership between levels is about *showing up with discernment, humility, and grace* — knowing when to challenge, when to champion, and when to just sit with your people in the mess. This tension won't go away. But it will shape you. And it just might be where your greatest growth begins.

Let's bring it all together

Final Thought:

Leadership isn't a staircase — it's a series of overlapping seasons. And no matter where you find yourself today — leading from the front, holding the middle, or setting the vision — the call is the same: *serve first*. As your reach expands, so does your opportunity to reflect the heart of servant leadership in every decision, conversation, and quiet moment in between.

What's Next

In the next chapter, we'll zoom out and look at how servant leadership impacts more than just relationships — it drives results. You'll explore how honoring people's worth creates healthier teams, stronger service, and lasting success. The research backs it. The stories prove it. Let's connect the dots between how we lead and what we achieve.

Chapter 7 Wrap-Up:
Scaling Servant Leadership

Key Takeaways:

- Servant leadership is needed at every level — but it must scale with your influence.

- Frontline leaders shape experience, mid-levels shape alignment, executives shape culture.

- The higher you go, the more people you serve.

- Presence > position. Listening > lecturing. Culture is shaped by what leaders tolerate or celebrate.

Reflection Questions:

1. Which level are you currently leading from — and are you bringing your Heart, Head, and Hands to it?

2. What mindsets or habits need to shift as your role expands?

3. What's one thing you could start (or stop) doing to better serve your team this week?

4. Where might your current leadership rhythm be drifting — and what's one way to reset this week?

Mini-Challenge:

This week, build a bridge in both directions. Encourage someone who leads you. Support someone who reports to you. That's how servant leaders grow their reach — not by climbing, but by connecting.

♦ The Priceless Punchline:

Q: Why did the department head bring snacks to the strategy meeting?
A: Because influence grows best when everyone's fed — literally and figuratively.

Notes *(Use this space to capture your thoughts, reactions, or action steps from this chapter)*

_____

_____

_____

_____

_____

_____

_____

_____

_____

_____

_____

_____

_____

"The true measure of leadership is how many lives you lift — not how high you climb." – Kevin Hall, Aspire

Chapter 8:

The Service-Profit Chain

Why employee experience drives organizational success – and how servant leadership fuels it all.[17]

Most leaders ask, '*How do we improve performance?*' But the real question is, *'How are our people?'* Because if your people are drained, no dashboard will save you.

A Brief History of the Service-Profit Chain[18]

The Service-Profit Chain isn't just a catchy phrase – it's a research-backed model that first emerged from Harvard Business School in the 1990s. Professors James Heskett, W. Earl Sasser, and Leonard Schlesinger introduced the concept in a 1994 Harvard Business Review article and later expanded on it in their book, The Service Profit Chain: *How Leading Companies Link Profit and Growth to Loyalty, Satisfaction, and Value.*[19]

Their research uncovered a clear, compelling pattern in top-performing organizations: when leaders invest in the employee experience, they ignite a chain reaction – increased employee satisfaction leads to better service delivery, which drives customer satisfaction, loyalty, and ultimately, profitability and growth.

The beauty of the model is in its simplicity: happy employees → happy customers → healthy business. But, as any leader knows, simple doesn't mean easy. The model challenges leaders to prioritize people and culture – not just performance metrics.

The Big Idea

Success – however you define it – comes from a strong culture fueled by highly satisfied, highly engaged employees. That's the essence of the Service-Profit Chain. It's not a warm-and-fuzzy ideal – it's a research-validated model that powers some of the most successful brands on the planet.[20]

At its core, the Service-Profit Chain explains how internal leadership decisions and practices impact employee experience, which in turn shapes customer experience and ultimately drives business results. In other words: treat your employees well, and they'll treat your customers well – and your business will thrive.[21]

Why This Chain Matters

Leaders often get distracted by the noise of numbers. Spreadsheets, dashboards, compliance metrics – all valuable, but none of them exist in a vacuum. Every number is the result of a process, and every process is carried out by a person. If your people aren't thriving, your numbers eventually won't either.

Unfortunately, many executives fall into the trap of performance-first leadership. They focus on outcomes without digging into the culture, systems, and daily experiences that drive those outcomes. Some even try to make up for weak employee experiences by showing up for a photo op or scheduling a brief site visit. Employees see right through it. Without authenticity, engagement suffers.

Organizations that thrive understand the deeper connection. They recognize that employees who feel seen, heard, and supported create customer experiences that delight and build loyalty.

Story: The Turnaround Call Center

One call center client we worked with had been stuck at a 30% customer problem-resolution rate for years. They held agents accountable to average call times, coached using recorded calls, and even threw occasional pizza parties. But engagement was low, and performance never improved.

When we pulled back the curtain, we saw a culture of neglect. Agents only received feedback when they made mistakes. There was no individual recognition, no personal development, and little to no investment in team morale. People felt like replaceable cogs in a machine, not valued contributors with potential.

We implemented a new approach: real-time coaching with positive reinforcement, individualized recognition, empowerment to resolve common issues without supervisor approval, and regular team-building activities. We trained supervisors to become encouragers, not enforcers, and they started catching people doing things right.

Within a year, engagement scores jumped 20%, and customer resolution scores hit 40% for the first time in 15 years. People felt seen. Customers felt heard. That's the Service-Profit Chain in action.[22]

But what stood out most wasn't just the metrics – it was the momentum. Agents who once stayed silent in meetings started sharing ideas. One even launched a "recognition board" to celebrate team wins, and another became a team lead within six months. The change in culture didn't just improve performance – it restored dignity, sparked initiative, and reminded leaders that when you invest in people, they show up differently. And when people show up differently, results follow.

The Chain Explained

The Service-Profit Chain

- Profitability & Growth
- Brand Loyalty
- Customer Behavior
- Customer Satisfaction
- Customer Experience
- Employee Behavior
- Employee Satisfaction
- Employee Experience
- Leadership

Think of the Service-Profit Chain like a ripple effect of leadership decisions. One link affects the next — and it all begins with how leaders show up. Let's walk through the links, starting from the bottom up:

1. Leadership

Everything starts with how leaders show up. Leadership sets the tone for communication, recognition, empowerment, training, and more. This includes frontline supervisors creating daily structure, middle managers reinforcing purpose, and executives shaping systems and policies that serve people well. Leaders create the...

2. Employee Experience

This is the day-to-day reality of what it feels like to work in your organization. It's shaped by psychological safety, communication, respect, trust, flexibility, tools, and how employees are treated when life gets messy. The experience determines...

3. Employee Satisfaction

When the experience is positive, people feel fulfilled and supported. They have what they need to succeed and know they are valued. This influences...

4. Employee Behavior

Satisfied employees show up differently. They're more engaged, innovative, collaborative, and resilient. They go the extra mile. And they create the...

5. Customer Experience

Customers feel the difference. They receive better service, more consistency, and often, more empathy. This drives...

6. Customer Satisfaction

As experiences improve, so do emotions. Customers feel loyalty, trust, and connection to the brand. This is what influences...

7. Customer Behavior

Satisfied customers return, spend more, refer others, and become brand advocates. And this, ladies and gentlemen, is what fuels **brand loyalty** and ultimately...

8. Growth & Profit

All of this feeds into business results: higher retention, lower turnover, stronger reputation, and long-term performance.

Servant Leadership as the Chain's Foundation

And at every link of the chain, servant leadership plays a pivotal role:

- Servant leaders invest in systems that enable people to thrive.

- They foster environments where feedback, recognition, and care are the norm.

- They empower employees to act in the best interests of customers.

- They prioritize long-term culture over short-term fixes.

A Tale of Two Approaches: Traditional vs. Servant Leadership

There are key distinctions between traditional leadership and servant leadership at every link in the Service-Profit Chain. Each row shows how a leader's approach shapes the employee experience, which then cascades outward – impacting customer relationships, brand loyalty, and ultimately, organizational growth.[23]

In the *traditional model*, leadership often begins with control and ends with pressure for performance. Employees are seen as resources to be managed, and the result is typically compliance, transactional customer relationships, and short-term gains.

In contrast, the *servant leadership model* flips the script. Leaders serve their teams first – coaching, equipping, and trusting them. This creates a culture where employees feel valued, customers feel genuinely cared for, and long-term loyalty drives sustainable success.

This chart invites you to reflect on how your leadership shows up at each link in the chain – and whether it reflects a mindset of managing or serving.

Managing vs. Serving:
Leadership Impact at Every Link

Link in Chain	Traditional Leadership	Servant Leadership
Leadership	Direct, control, manage	Equip, empower, support
Employee Experience	Uniform, process-driven	Personalized, human-centered
Employee Satisfaction	Low priority, assumed	Measured, nurtured
Employee Behavior	Compliance-oriented	Commitment-oriented
Customer Experience	Transactional	Relational
Customer Satisfaction	Surface-level metrics	Emotional connection
Customer Behavior	Focus on retention tactics	Focus on loyalty through value
Growth & Profit	Squeeze more from less	Build more by serving better

Case Study:

Chick-fil-A – Serving Employees to Serve Customers [24]

Chick-fil-A doesn't just serve meals — it serves people. And it starts with how they treat their own. Their remarkable success in the fast-food industry stems from its unwavering commitment to an employee-first culture, exemplifying the service-profit chain. By prioritizing the well-being and development of its employees, the company fosters exceptional customer experiences, leading to impressive financial performance.[25] What's their secret sauce? Let's break down the key ingredients that fuel Chick-fil-A's people-first success.

1. Purpose-Driven Culture

At the heart of Chick-fil-A's operations is a clear and compelling purpose: "To glorify God by being a faithful steward of all that is entrusted to us." This mission translates into a culture that values every individual, ensuring that employees feel respected and empowered. Such an environment encourages staff to extend genuine care to customers, enhancing service quality. [26]

2. Strategic Hiring and Comprehensive Training

Chick-fil-A emphasizes hiring individuals who align with its values, focusing on character and cultural fit over mere technical skills. New team members undergo extensive training that covers customer service excellence, food preparation, and cleanliness standards. Continuous development opportunities ensure that employees are well-equipped to deliver exceptional service consistently. [27]

3. Innovative Profit-Sharing Model

Unique among fast-food franchises, Chick-fil-A implements a profit-sharing arrangement where operators split net profits 50/50 with the company. This model fosters a sense of shared responsibility and incentivizes operators to invest in their teams, leading to higher employee satisfaction and retention. [28]

4. Tangible Employee Benefits

Beyond competitive wages, Chick-fil-A offers meaningful benefits that address employees' needs. These include daily free meals, childcare support, and substantial scholarship programs. Such perks demonstrate the company's genuine investment in its employees' personal and professional growth. [29]

5. Exceptional Customer Service Leading to Financial Success

The positive employee experience at Chick-fil-A translates directly into superior customer service. The company consistently ranks highest in customer satisfaction within the fast-food industry. This dedication to service excellence contributes to impressive financial metrics, with Chick-fil-A averaging $9.3 million in sales per standalone restaurant, surpassing many competitors. [30]

Chick-fil-A's approach underscores a fundamental principle: investing in employees creates a ripple effect that enhances customer satisfaction and drives profitability. Their model serves as a compelling example of how servant leadership and a people-centric culture can yield outstanding business outcomes.[31]

Chick-fil-A's success isn't magic – it's modeled leadership in action. And you don't need a drive-thru to drive this kind of culture.

This same principle holds true at companies like Ritz-Carlton, SAS, and Costco – where employee experience is directly tied to customer delight and long-term profitability.

Servant leadership isn't just a feel-good philosophy – it's a proven growth strategy. When leaders invest in people first, results follow. Chapter 8 showed us how the Service-Profit Chain flips traditional leadership upside-down, placing employee experience at the heart of organizational success. Whether you're leading a team of 3 or a company of 3,000, the message is clear: take care of your people, and they'll take care of everything else. Culture doesn't happen by accident – it's shaped by the daily choices leaders make.[32]

So remember...

Don't just manage the numbers. Multiply the impact by serving the people.

Chapter 8 Wrap-Up: The Service-Profit Chain[33]

Key Takeaways

- The Service-Profit Chain shows how employee experience drives customer satisfaction – and ultimately, organizational success.[34]

- Every link in the chain begins with leadership decisions: how we hire, train, recognize, and care for our people.

- Servant leadership isn't just morally right – it's strategically wise.

- Organizations thrive when they stop managing for output and start leading for people.

Reflection Questions

5. Which link in the Service-Profit Chain is the strongest in your organization? Which is the weakest?[35]

6. How does your team's day-to-day experience impact the way they serve others?

7. Are your current leadership systems and behaviors building loyalty – or burning people out?

8. What's one leadership practice you could change this month to strengthen the employee experience?

Mini-Challenge

Ask your team: What builds trust here? What breaks it? Then choose one small way to make it better — and follow through this week.

◆ The Priceless Punchline

Q: Why did the company start serving cookies in the break-room?

A: Because happy employees crumble less under pressure.

Notes *(Use this space to capture your thoughts, reactions, or action steps from this chapter)*

"Your employees come first. And if you treat your employees right, guess what? Your customers come back, and that makes your shareholders happy. Start with employees and the rest follows from that." –Herb Kelleher, CEO and co-founder of Southwest Airlines

Chapter 9:

Developing a Servant Leader
*Practical steps to grow in the 12 core
servant leadership traits.*

*Leadership isn't just about who you are today — it's about who
you're becoming tomorrow.*

Now that you've taken the Priceless Leadership Self-Assessment (chapter 6), you might be wondering: What do I do with
this? This chapter is your answer.

Here's where we move from insight to action.

Servant leadership is not a fixed identity or personality trait. It's
a way of leading that grows as you grow. These 12 servant leadership traits aren't just buzzwords or abstract virtues – they are
the building blocks of trust, influence, and impact. This chapter
will help you deepen your understanding of each one and develop a personalized growth plan that works for your context.

The 12 traits are broken down into the three different layers of
leadership: *who you are (Heart), how you think (Head), and what
you do (Hands).*

But before we jump into the traits, let's explore a simple but
powerful professional development strategy.

How Leaders Grow: The 70-20-10 Approach

Most leaders don't need another leadership class. They need meaningful, personalized development. And not the kind that just fills your bookshelf — but the kind that actually shifts how you lead.

That's where the 70-20-10 model comes in. It's a research-backed framework for how adults grow best:

70% Learning by Doing (on-the-job experiences)

20% Learning with Others (coaching, mentoring, feedback)

10% Learning through Training (books, webinars, podcasts)

Let's break that down with a hypothetical situation:

Imagine your 16-year-old son just finished his driver's ed class. He's read the handbook, watched the safety videos, and passed the quiz. Now he's asking for the car keys and a full tank of gas — because he's planning a solo road trip from Orlando to Seattle tomorrow.

After all, he "knows how to drive" now... right?

Cue the parental panic!!!

That's the danger of relying too much on the 10%. A class can introduce you to a skill, but it can't develop it. Real growth happens in the driver's seat.

Think about your own experience learning to drive:

- 10% most likely came from formal instruction.
- 20% came from coaching and feedback (maybe from a brave parent or patient instructor).
- 70% came from actually driving – parallel parking on a crowded city street, finding the wipers in a downpour, missing an exit and figuring it out.

Leadership development works the same way. Books and classes might give you clarity – but real growth happens behind the wheel. Confidence, character, and conviction are formed through the messy, beautiful, real-life moments of leadership.

That's why developing the 12 servant leadership traits isn't about consuming more content. It's about creating a growth plan rooted in experience, reflection, and community.

A quick word of advice: Don't try to grow in everything at once. As you read through the 12 traits, keep an eye out for the *one* that resonates most right now. Just one. Leadership development isn't a sprint — it's a series of intentional steps. And focusing on one trait at a time allows you to go deeper, see progress, and avoid burnout.

You'll build a simple growth plan for that trait at the end of this chapter. Once that habit becomes part of your leadership rhythm, come back and pick the next one. Slow growth is strong growth.

Before we dive in, grab your assessment results from Chapter 6. Which domains – Heart, Head, or Hands – stood out as strengths? Which ones stretched you? Keep those scores close as we explore each trait. They'll help you zero in on where to begin.

The 12 Servant Leadership Traits

As we walk through each trait, we'll look at four key areas:

• **Definition** – what the trait means

• **Why it matters** – why this trait is essential for servant leaders

• **How it looks in practice** – real-world behaviors and examples

• **Ways to grow (70-20-10)** – sample practical steps to develop each trait

---

Great leadership starts from the inside out – and the *Heart* traits form the foundation. These traits shape your character, build trust, and influence how others experience your presence. This is where servant leadership begins: with who you are.

♥ HEART

Empathy

Definition: Understanding and sharing the feelings and perspectives of others.
Why It Matters: Builds trust and psychological safety, especially in times of change or tension.

How It Looks in Practice: Active listening, checking in during stress, showing compassion in decision-making.
Grow With 70-20-10:

- **70%:** Begin every 1:1 with a personal check-in. Practice listening without interrupting or fixing.

- **20%:** Ask for feedback from peers on your listening and emotional presence.

- **10%:** Read The Empathy Edge, watch Brené Brown's TED Talk on empathy, or take an EQ course.[36]

Humility

Definition: A willingness to admit limitations, seek input, and share credit.
Why It Matters: Keeps egos in check, strengthens collaboration, and invites wisdom.
How It Looks in Practice: Owning mistakes, welcoming feedback, elevating others' ideas.
Grow With 70-20-10:

- **70%:** Share a mistake and what you learned. Publicly recognize someone else's contribution.

- **20%:** Ask a mentor to point out blind spots.

- **10%:** Read Humilitas or study Philippians 2 on Christ's example of humility.

Integrity

Definition: Doing what's right – even when it's hard or when no one sees.
Why It Matters: Builds credibility and sets the moral tone for the team.
How It Looks in Practice: Keeping your word, addressing wrongs directly, modeling ethics.
Grow With 70-20-10:

- **70%:** Speak up when something's unethical or misaligned. Keep all promises, large or small.

- **20%:** Share ethical dilemmas with a trusted peer and discuss options.

- **10%:** Take a business ethics class or reflect on Psalm 15.

Compassion

Definition: Responding to others with care, patience, and kindness.
Why It Matters: Builds connection and emotional safety, especially during hardship.
How It Looks in Practice: Offering grace, being present in pain, creating space for healing.
Grow With 70-20-10:

- **70%:** Practice being fully present when someone shares a struggle.

- **20%:** Ask a teammate when they last felt truly supported – then listen deeply.

- **10%:** Read The Art of Compassion or reflect on the Good Samaritan (Luke 10).

Next comes the mindset of a servant leader – the *Head* traits. These traits influence how you process information, make decisions, and lead with wisdom and clarity. They bridge your inner values with your outward leadership.

 HEAD

Vision

Definition: The ability to articulate a compelling and hopeful future.
Why It Matters: Motivates and aligns teams to move forward with purpose.
How It Looks in Practice: Tying team goals to mission, setting direction during uncertainty.
Grow With 70-20-10:

- **70%:** Lead a vision casting conversation with your team.

- **20%:** Share your vision with a peer or mentor for feedback.

- **10%:** Read Start With Why by Simon Sinek or take a strategic leadership course.

Wisdom

Definition: Applying truth and discernment to decisions and relationships.
Why It Matters: Helps leaders slow down, consider consequences, and make sound judgments.
How It Looks in Practice: Asking good questions, listening well, weighing long-term outcomes.

Grow With 70-20-10:

- **70%:** Pause before responding to tough situations. Document what you're learning after decisions.

- **20%:** Meet with a mentor for advice and processing.

- **10%:** Read Proverbs 4:7 or attend a decision-making workshop.

Accountability

Definition: Taking ownership for results, behaviors, and commitments.

Why It Matters: Builds trust and fairness while improving performance.

How It Looks in Practice: Following through, having hard conversations, setting clear expectations.

Grow With 70-20-10:

- **70%:** Track commitments visually and close loops. Address performance issues early.

- **20%:** Ask your team how you're doing on follow-through.

- **10%:** Take a feedback or performance management course.

Discernment

Definition: Pausing to reflect, pray (if that's part of your practice), and seek insight before acting or advising.

Why It Matters: Prevents reactionary decisions and encourages spirit-led, thoughtful leadership.

How It Looks in Practice: Seeking input, creating white space to listen, resisting urgency culture.
Grow With 70-20-10:

- **70%:** Build margin before big decisions. Ask, "What's the wise thing to do?"

- **20%:** Invite a mentor to pray or reflect with you on a decision.

- **10%:** Read The Listening Life or study Proverbs 3:5–6.

Finally, the *Hands* bring servant leadership to life. These traits reflect your actions – how you serve, empower, and steward people and resources. It's where your values show up in how you lead every day.

✦ HANDS

Service

Definition: Meeting the needs of others, even when inconvenient or unnoticed.
Why It Matters: Embodies Christ-like leadership and builds loyalty.
How It Looks in Practice: Helping without being asked, stepping in behind the scenes.
Grow With 70-20-10:

- **70%:** Ask "How can I serve you this week?" at the start of meetings.

- **20%:** Interview a leader known for their servant heart.

- **10%:** Read The Servant by James Hunter or study John 13.[37]

Empowerment

Definition: Equipping and trusting others to own their work and grow.

Why It Matters: Grows confidence, builds capacity, and supports healthy delegation.

How It Looks in Practice: Assigning real responsibility, coaching through challenges.

Grow With 70-20-10:

- **70%:** Let go of a task and coach someone else to lead it.

- **20%:** Ask a peer for feedback on your delegation habits.

- **10%:** Take a coaching course or watch a coaching demo series.

Stewardship

Definition: Managing time, resources, and influence wisely for the good of others.

Why It Matters: Ensures that leaders remain trustworthy and focused on what matters.

How It Looks in Practice: Budgeting well, honoring people's time, protecting team focus.

Grow With 70-20-10:

- **70%:** Audit your calendar and team workload to align with mission.

- **20%:** Ask a peer how they prioritize competing demands.

- **10%:** Study nonprofit leadership, time management, or biblical stewardship.

Courage

Definition: Boldly doing what's right even when it's difficult or scary.
Why It Matters: Enables honest conversations and principled leadership.
How It Looks in Practice: Giving difficult feedback, naming hard truths with grace.
Grow With 70-20-10:

- **70%:** Initiate a conversation you've been avoiding this week.

- **20%:** Role-play tough conversations with a peer or coach.

- **10%:** Read Dare to Lead or take a courageous leadership course.

Your Personalized Leadership Development Plan

Now that you've explored all 12 traits, it's time to choose your growth path.

Start by selecting *one* trait that stood out to you — maybe it's a strength you want to deepen, or a stretch area that's calling for your attention in this season.

Then, for that one trait, map out a simple 70-20-10 plan using the template in the back of the book — or just grab a blank sheet of paper. No need for perfection here. The goal is momentum, not mastery.

Here's how to get started:

- *70% Learning by Doing*
What specific action or habit will you practice in your day-to-day work?

- *20% Learning with Others*
  Who can you learn from, get feedback from, or reflect with?

- *10% Learning through Training*
  What will you read, watch, or attend to deepen your insight?

- *Goal & Deadline*
  What will success look like, and by when?

Example: Growing in Courage

- *Trait*: Courage

- *70%*: Initiate a feedback conversation I've been avoiding this week.

- *20%*: Ask a peer to role-play the conversation with me.

- *10%*: Watch a TED Talk or read an article on crucial conversations.

- *Goal*: Have the conversation by next Friday and debrief afterward with my peer.

Start small. Go deep. And come back for the next trait when you're ready. Servant leadership is a journey — one brave step at a time.

Before you begin writing your plan, here's a real-world reminder of what it looks like when servant leadership is lived out — not just as theory, but in everyday business decisions, training, and culture.

The Container Store offers a powerful case study in what happens when companies develop the Heart, Head, and Hands of their leaders at every level — and they've built a thriving workplace by doing exactly that.

Case Study:
The Container Store – Leading with Love and Logic[38]

The Container Store has long been a darling of workplace culture advocates, and it's easy to see why. Built on the philosophy of "1=3" (one great employee is as productive as three good ones), the company invests heavily in the training, support, and well-being of its people.[39]

Full-time employees receive more than *260 hours of training* in their first year – compared to the retail industry average of 7 hours. But this isn't just product training. The Container Store trains employees in emotional intelligence, communication, customer empathy, and values-driven decision-making.[40]

Leaders at The Container Store are taught to lead with empathy, and their management training includes modules on active listening, empowering others, and creating a psychologically safe environment. One leader shared, "We don't ask, 'How can this person help the business?' We ask, 'How can the business help this person thrive?'"[41]

This people-first approach has earned the company accolades like Fortune's "Best Companies to Work For" and consistently high customer satisfaction scores. Even during difficult seasons in the retail industry, The Container Store's employee retention remained strong, thanks to its focus on servant leadership principles.[42]

When people are treated like they matter, they respond with loyalty, creativity, and excellence. The Container Store reminds us that servant leadership isn't soft – it's smart.[43]

The Container Store shows us what's possible. But you don't need a corporate budget to build a culture of servant leadership — just a clear commitment to grow, one moment at a time.

Servant leadership isn't developed in a day — it's forged in the daily grind of meetings, deadlines, and moments that test your patience. But as you've seen in this chapter, it can be developed. You now have the tools to start growing in the traits that matter most. Whether you're just beginning your leadership journey or refining your impact at the executive level, small, intentional steps can lead to transformation — in you and in your team.

In the next chapter, we'll take this one step further. You'll learn how to put servant leadership into practice in the rhythms of everyday leadership — from feedback to decision-making to delegation. Because leadership development doesn't just happen in workshops. It happens in the moments that matter most.

You've built the foundation. You've learned the way. Now let's live it out — one moment, one decision, one act of leadership at a time.

Chapter 9 Wrap-Up: Developing the Heart, Head, and Hands of a Servant Leader

Key Takeaways

- Servant leadership is formed through daily choices – and developed across three key domains: Heart (who you are), Head (how you think), and Hands (what you do).

- Each of the 12 servant leadership traits can be learned, practiced, and strengthened over time.

- The 70-20-10 model helps you turn awareness into action through real experiences, mentoring, and intentional learning.

- The best leaders are always growing – because leadership is never a finished product.

- You don't need to master all 12 traits overnight. Just start. Pick one. Practice it. Watch what happens. Leadership grows with each choice you make.

Reflection Questions

1. Which servant leadership traits come naturally to you? Which ones stretch you?

2. How are you intentionally developing in each domain – Heart, Head, and Hands?

3. What's one trait you want others to associate with your leadership legacy?

Mini-Challenge

Pick one trait that you want to grow in over the next 30 days. Write a simple 70-20-10 plan for it. Then share your focus with someone who can help you stay accountable.

◆ The Priceless Punchline

Q: Why did the leader go to Home Depot?
A: To pick up more tools for their heart, head, and hands.

Notes (*Use this space to capture your thoughts, reactions, or action steps from this chapter*)

_____

_____

_____

_____

_____

_____

_____

_____

_____

_____

_____

"How you do anything is how you do everything."
– T. Harv Eker

Part III:

PUTTING IT INTO PRACTICE

You've now walked the path of the servant leader.

You've explored the mindset. You've seen the model. You've felt the impact.

Now comes the question that matters most: *Will you live it out?*

This section is where theory becomes testimony – where everything you've learned gets tested in real-life moments:

In tomorrow morning's meeting.

In your next one-on-one.

In that tough conversation you've been avoiding.

These next chapters are practical. They're personal.

They're not about what you know – they're about what you do.

Because leadership isn't something we admire.

It's something we practice.

One moment. One person. One ripple at a time.

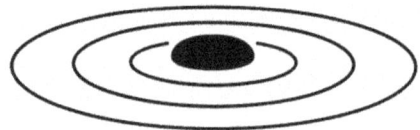

"Your influence is measured not by your position, but by the stories people tell about how you made them feel."— Adapted from Maya Angelou's legacy and the servant leadership ethos[44]

Chapter 10:

The Ripple Effect

Small Acts of Leadership. Big Waves of Impact.

From Title to Tidal Wave

This chapter is all about activation – the small steps, habits, and unseen choices that bring servant leadership to life. And it begins with a truth that may surprise you:

You don't need a title to shape culture.

Leadership isn't reserved for people with the biggest offices or the loudest voices. Leadership is influence – and every action you take sends ripples outward.

A Pebble in the Water

You've probably heard the metaphor before. A pebble, dropped into still water, sends ripples outward – far beyond where it first landed.

So does leadership.

You may never fully know how a single conversation, decision, or moment of dignity affects someone. But rest assured: it does. Sometimes, in ways you won't discover for years – if ever.

I once worked with a woman who was deeply disappointed after not being selected for a promotion at our resort. As her leader, I had chosen another candidate – not because she wasn't qualified, but because the role required complementary skills that the other candidate brought to the team.

I avoided a follow-up conversation, hoping she'd "bounce back" with time. But when I finally sat down with her, I discovered something unexpected: she wasn't just disappointed – she was questioning her worth.

"I'll never get ahead here," she said, *"because of how I look."*

That wasn't something I saw coming. But in that moment, I had a choice: minimize her pain, or sit with her in it. I chose the latter. I clarified the *real* reason behind the decision and expressed *genuine* belief in her leadership future.

Fast forward – she went on to become the Assistant GM... then GM... of that very resort.

That one conversation — the one I almost skipped — rippled in ways I never expected.

Small Acts, Long Echoes

It's tempting to think leadership happens in quarterly meetings, annual strategy decks, or performance reviews. But some of the greatest leadership moments happen in the margins – unplanned, unseen by most, but unforgettable to the person it touched.

Here are a few examples of those small, sacred moments — the ones that leave a lasting imprint:

- Stopping everything to give someone your full, undivided attention

- Canceling an important meeting to be present for a team member going through something hard

- Handwriting a thank-you card and mailing it to an employee's home

- Sending cookies to a team member's family as a thank-you for their support

- Giving someone a stretch project that shows you believe in them

- Telling them to go – to the hospital, to their kid's recital, to be where they're needed

- Publicly giving credit to someone whose contribution made the difference

These aren't performance metrics. These are leadership imprints – little actions that whisper, *"You matter."*

It only takes one intentional act to change how someone sees themselves – and sometimes, even how they lead. Just ask the people at Southwest Airlines.

Case Study:
From a President's Pen to a Culture of Care

At *Southwest Airlines*, servant leadership isn't just a mission statement – it's woven into the culture. One story often shared inside the company is about *Colleen Barrett*, Southwest's former President, who was known for writing thousands of personal notes to employees over the years.

During a routine flight, a flight attendant noticed that a passenger with special needs was becoming anxious. The attendant, named Jamie, took it upon herself and sat with the passenger during boarding, held her hand during takeoff, and helped her feel calm throughout the flight.

Jamie didn't do it for attention – it was just who she was. A fellow crew member mentioned it in a post-flight report sent to

Southwest's leadership team – including (you guessed it) Colleen.

Later that week, she received a handwritten note from Colleen, thanking her not only for what she did, but *how* she did it. "*You didn't just serve a passenger,*" Colleen wrote. "*You affirmed her worth. That's what makes Southwest different.*"

That one note changed how Jamie saw her role. It reminded her that leadership isn't about tasks – it's about affirming someone's worth. She started mentoring others and eventually became part of the onboarding team for new hires – teaching them not just how to do the job, but how to lead with heart.

Years later, she still keeps Colleen's note in her locker.

Why It Matters:

Colleen could've just read the report and moved on. But she paused, responded, and created a ripple – one that multiplied the servant leadership culture Southwest is known for.

Leadership as Identity-Shaping

I often remind leaders of this quiet truth:

Sometimes, you're the first person in someone's life to treat them like they're truly priceless.

That kind of moment isn't just meaningful — it's transformational. It can shift a person's story long after the moment has passed.

Many people weren't raised to believe they have value. They've spent their lives hustling for worth — hoping to be seen, approved of, or enough.

A servant leader does more than manage performance. They affirm identity. They help rewrite internal stories. They become one of the few voices that whisper:

You belong.
You are valued.
You have something unique to offer.
You are not forgotten.
You are priceless.

That's more than motivation. That's healing.
And it often starts in the workplace — when a leader decides to *see* someone differently.

And when leaders consistently treat people as priceless, the ripple doesn't stop with individuals. Over time, it begins to shape the culture — not through posters or perks, but through presence.

Culture Isn't a Campaign

Culture is the outcome of what leaders *do* every day – especially when they think no one is watching.

You can roll out new benefits, hand out branded mugs, and build a flashy orientation program – but if your team members feel like your door is always closed (literally or figuratively), they'll learn what culture really means here.

As I like to say: *"Culture is created intentionally or unintentionally. Either way, it's created."*

Here are just a few examples of culture-shaping behaviors:

- Greeting people by name every morning (or not)

- Being the first to admit a mistake

- Staying late to help when someone's overwhelmed

- Bringing a "Warning!" moment to the surface – gently but directly

- Creating team rituals that reflect your values (e.g., High-five Fridays, weekly devotionals, team Lunch and Learns, etc.)

- Listening first, even when you're sure you're right

These small acts (and others like them), repeated over time, shape how people feel — and who they believe they are. But sometimes, a single moment can change everything.

There's a story that captures this perfectly, and even if you've never opened a Bible, it still speaks volumes.

The Jesus Ripple

Sometimes the most powerful leadership moment... isn't in a boardroom. It's at a well. One of the most transformational ripple moments in history began not with a speech, but with a conversation.

A woman, burdened by shame and isolation, walks alone to a well in the heat of the day — a time others avoided. She'd been cast aside by her community because of her complicated past and personal relationships. In their eyes, she didn't measure up.

But then she meets someone different.
A Jewish teacher named Jesus — someone she never expected to notice her.

He doesn't look away. He doesn't judge.
Instead, he talks with her. Asks her for a drink — a small act, but in that culture, it carried weight. It meant: *you're worthy of dignity.*

He listens. He knows her story.
And instead of turning away, he leans in with kindness.

That conversation changed her life.
She ran back to her village saying, *"Come meet someone who truly saw me."*
And they came.

That's the ripple.
One moment of worth restored.
One life seen and lifted — that went on to lift others.

What Ripples Are You Creating?

"Be the change you wish to see in the world." —Gandhi

The ripple didn't start with a miracle. It started with a moment of presence — one person choosing to listen, to care, to lead with compassion. You don't need to be famous, powerful, or perfect to create that kind of ripple. You just need to be willing.

The habits you live — not just the words you say — are what ripple into others.

Gandhi once turned down a mother who asked him to tell her son to stop eating sugar. *"Come back in two weeks,"* he told her.

When she returned, he looked the boy in the eye and said, *"Stop eating sugar."*

The mother was grateful yet confused. *"Why couldn't you have said that two weeks ago?"*

Gandhi replied, *"Because I had to stop eating sugar first."*

Ripples begin with you. Your life, your habits, your walk.

You don't need to be perfect. But you do need to be intentional. You don't need a title. You just need to start dropping pebbles.

Ripples don't require grand gestures. Sometimes, it's just a hallway moment. A few words. A look that says, I see you. And in that instant, something shifts.

What Were They Thinking?
"The Fork in the Road" by Hannah B.

It was a rough week. I was behind on a deadline, struggling at home, and starting to feel invisible at work. I thought no one noticed – or cared.

But then, as I was walking to the break room, our divisional VP – who I thought didn't even know me – stopped me in the hallway. He looked me in the eyes and said, "*Hey, Hannah! I just want to say how impressed I am by the work you are doing on the project... it's going to make a big impact.*"

Reflection Questions:

1. What was Hannah thinking at this moment?
2. How did this affect Hannah's feelings and emotions?
3. What impact did this have on Hannah's behavior and performance?

(*Turn to page 153 to read Hannah's real reflections.*)

Lessons from the Ripple

It wasn't a meeting. It wasn't a memo. It was a passing comment in a hallway – and it stayed with her. Big change doesn't always come from big moments. Most of the time, it's the small, everyday choices – how we speak to someone, how we show up, how we listen – that echo the loudest in the hearts of others.

In this chapter, we saw how servant leadership doesn't need a spotlight. It just needs a heart that sees people as priceless and a mindset that's willing to show up with love, even when no one's watching.

Like a single pebble dropped into a pond, your actions create waves. A moment of kindness, a word of encouragement, or a pause to truly listen – those are the ripples that shift culture, restore dignity, and change lives .

And remember: you don't have to fix everything. You just have to drop the pebble — and trust that your small act of leadership may affirm someone's priceless value in ways you'll never fully see.

In the next chapter, we'll follow two leaders through a single day – and see how their choices create very different ripples. One inspires trust. The other leaves a wake of damage. The difference? It's not their position. It's how they lead in the little moments.

Chapter 10 Wrap-Up: The Ripple Effect

Key Takeaways

- Leadership isn't always loud. Often, the greatest impact comes from quiet, unseen acts of care.

- Small, intentional behaviors can shape how people see themselves – and how they show up in the world.

- Culture is created in the margins: hallway conversations, how we respond to stress, and whether we choose empathy over efficiency.

- Servant leaders ripple out hope, healing, and belonging, one conversation at a time.

Reflection Questions

1. What small moment of leadership has stayed with you the longest? Why?

2. Who needs to feel seen, heard, or encouraged by you this week?

3. Are your leadership ripples reinforcing dignity – or performance pressure?

Mini-Challenge

Think of someone who may not realize the impact they've had on you. Write them a short note of appreciation. Then drop another pebble: affirm someone's worth in a conversation this week — especially if they don't expect it. You might even inspire a ripple you'll never see.

◈ The Priceless Punchline

Q: Why did the pebble apply for a promotion?
A: It knew it was making waves – even if no one saw the splash.

Notes *(Use this space to capture your thoughts, reactions, or action steps from this chapter)*

----

*"Drop a pebble in the water: just a splash, and it is gone...
But there's half-a-hundred ripples circling on and on and
on." – James W. Foley*

A Tale of Two Leaders

A day in the life of two very different leaders.

Before we begin – a confession: I love stories. Jesus did too. His most profound lessons weren't lectures; they were parables – simple, vivid stories packed with eternal truth.

In that same spirit, let's look at a modern-day parable: the day in the life of two leaders – Lucy and Lee.

Both serve as Director of Operations. But how they lead – and the ripples they leave behind – couldn't be more different.

Let's begin with the one who made leadership all about *them*.

The Day in the Life of Lucy
(I was going to name her Lucifer but decided to dial it back a notch.)

6:45 AM
Smash. That's the snooze button for the third time. Lucy finally drags herself out of bed, muttering about her team's incompetence and the endless meetings ahead. No real morning routine, unless you count a half-cup of lukewarm coffee, a cigarette, and a few rounds of online poker while the news plays in the background.

She checks her email. Three minor issues already. *"Figures."*

8:50 AM
Lucy pulls into the front parking spot labeled *"Director of Ops."* She made the Facilities team paint her name on it. Power move.

9:00 AM
She walks into the building and bypasses the front desk without a glance. Heads straight to her office, shuts the door, and fires off three curt emails.

10:06 AM
Team meeting. She's late. She walks in, says nothing about the delay, and jumps into the numbers. No greeting. No wins celebrated. No faces acknowledged.

Someone mentions a process issue. Lucy interrupts, blames a supervisor, and says, *"Figure it out. We don't have time for this nonsense."*

11:30 AM
An employee swings by to ask for guidance on a customer complaint. Lucy rolls her eyes, says, *"That's not my job,"* and reminds them to read the policy manual.

11:45 AM
Lunch break. Lucy grabs her purse and heads to that new steak

place across town. She doesn't invite anyone. Why would she? She needs a break – from *them*.

2:00 PM
Critical strategy meeting. High pressure. Lucy dominates the room, talks over others, and pushes her own agenda. When a peer raises a concern, she cuts them off: *"We're not here to debate. We're here to execute."*

4:45 PM
She packs up and leaves without saying goodbye. The door slams. Echoes.

Same title, same pressures — but let's take a look at a leader who flips the script.

The Day in the Life of Lee

5:30 AM
The alarm goes off. Lee wakes up, stretches, and spends 10 quiet minutes in prayer and reflection. He eats a healthy breakfast, reviews his calendar, and walks the dog while listening to a leadership podcast. He blocks out time later for a career conversation with one of his team members.

7:50 AM
Lee pulls into the last row of the parking lot. More steps, sure – but it frees up spots for guests and teammates. It's a small way to put others first.

8:00 AM
As Lee walks in, he greets people by name. *"How's your daughter doing, Miguel?"* *"Thanks again for jumping in on that project, Maria."*

He genuinely listens. Smiles. Encourages.

9:00 AM

Team meeting. Lee starts with a quick win from the floor staff. He thanks everyone for their effort and invites input on a few challenges. "*What do you think we should try?*" he asks. Heads nod. Ideas fly. Ownership grows.

11:00 AM

A frontline employee drops by with a customer issue. Lee stops typing, turns fully toward them, and asks questions. "*How can I help you think this through?*"

They leave with clarity and confidence.

12:00 PM

Lee invites two team members to lunch. He asks what's working and what's not. He takes notes. He thanks them. They feel seen.

2:00 PM

Big strategy meeting. Lee comes prepared but open. He affirms good ideas, asks thoughtful questions, and credits others often. His calm, collaborative presence raises the room's energy.

5:15 PM

Before leaving, Lee walks through the floor. He checks in with a few team members, offers encouragement, and asks, "*Is there anything I can do for you before I head out?*"

Then he reviews tomorrow's schedule, blocks out time for what matters most, and sends a short note to someone celebrating their work anniversary.

He prays over his team on the drive home.

Three Months Later...
Lucy's Department:

Employee turnover up 32% year-over-year

Customer satisfaction scores dropped 18%

Anonymous feedback from employee survey: *"Toxic culture. I'm just surviving."*

Lee's Department:

Employee engagement at all-time high

Internal promotions up 40%

Anonymous feedback: *"I feel known. I feel safe. I do my best work here."*

Lessons from the Tale of Two Leaders

This modern-day parable gives us a powerful window into how two leaders – faced with the same pressures – produced very different outcomes.

Lucy led with pressure, performance, and pride. She controlled instead of coached, reacted instead of reflected, and missed the opportunity to build trust and inspire her team.

Lee led with empathy, clarity, and courage. He focused on people, created space for others to shine, and modeled what it means to lead from the inside out. His leadership wasn't just about getting results – it was about reminding people they mattered.

Their stories remind us that leadership isn't about a title or task list – it's about how we treat people when it matters most.

Every day, we write a story with our leadership. Whether it's marked by frustration or fulfillment is up to us. So ask yourself — what story are you writing with your leadership today?

And hey...
Don't be a Lucy. Be a Lee, duh!

(Get it? Be a Lee-duh. It's how my New Englanders say "leader.")

Chapter 11 Wrap-Up: A Tale of Two Leaders

Key Takeaways

- Leadership behavior shapes workplace culture – every day, in every interaction.

- People-first leadership builds trust, motivation, and team cohesion.

- The same situation can produce wildly different outcomes depending on a leader's mindset and habits.

- The habits we choose to practice (or neglect) write the story of our leadership.

Reflection Questions

1. Which leader in the parable felt more familiar to you – and why?

2. What habits or behaviors from Lee do you want to emulate or strengthen?

3. What is one unhealthy leadership habit you're ready to let go of?

Mini-Challenge

Write your own "day in the life" script. Journal a short reflection imagining how you want your best day as a leader to look – from how you greet your team to how you handle setbacks. Then live it.

The Priceless Punchline

Q: What's a bad leader's favorite type of exercise?
A: Jumping to conclusions and running meetings that could've been emails.

Notes *(Use this space to capture your thoughts, reactions, or action steps from this chapter)*

_____

_____

_____

_____

_____

_____

_____

_____

_____

_____

_____

_____

_____

_____

"Sow a thought, reap an action; sow an action, reap a habit; sow a habit, reap a character; sow a character, reap a destiny." – Stephen R. Covey

Chapter 12:

Your Leadership Legacy

The story you're writing. The lives you're shaping.

Legacy Isn't Later. It's Now.

When we hear the word "legacy," we often imagine something written years from now. An epitaph. A tribute. A retirement speech. But the truth is, your leadership legacy is being written every day. It's the sum of your daily decisions, conversations, and even your silence. It shows up in how people talk about you when you're not in the room. It shows up in the stories they tell – or don't.

Legacy is shaped by how you made people feel, what you helped them believe about themselves, and whether they left your presence more whole – or more weary.

So, let me ask: if someone gave your team a blank page and asked them to write a few sentences about your impact, what would they write?

Invisible Imprints

Some of the greatest leadership legacies are invisible. They don't show up on a dashboard or get measured in KPIs. But they are no less real.

They show up in the confidence of a team member who finally spoke up in a meeting – because you made them feel heard.

They show up in a former employee who chased a new dream – because you reminded them of their worth when they forgot.

They show up in the family of your team member – who experienced more peace at home because their loved one was treated with dignity and not diminished at work.

Leadership isn't just about what you build. It's about what you leave behind in people.

What people remember most isn't your productivity – it's your presence. Not your checklist, but your character. And sometimes, the smallest act – a listening ear, a second chance, a genuine thank you – can ripple further than you ever imagined.

One Final Story

She wasn't my top performer. Not at first.

She was thoughtful, consistent, smart, and kind – but also hesitant. She held back in meetings. Downplayed her ideas. You could see the spark in her, but something inside was dimmed – a quiet voice that whispered, *"You're not ready. Don't stand out."*

I made it my mission to reflect something different. I listened. Encouraged. Coached. I helped her explore an opportunity outside our team – one that stretched her, aligned with her strengths, and scared her just enough to mean something.

She said yes. And something shifted.

She found her voice. She leaned in. She grew in confidence – and not just professionally. Her light got brighter in every part of her life.

Years later, she reached out and said, *"You didn't just see what I was good at – you helped me believe I had something to offer."*

That's when it hit me: she wasn't just doing well... she was becoming *that* kind of leader for someone else.

And that's the kind of legacy that never shows up on a dashboard – but lives on in stories, in ripple effects, in someone else's rising confidence.

I've seen it time and time again. Sometimes it's a text, years later. Sometimes it's a wedding I get to officiate (I've done more than a few). And every now and then, it's a moment where someone says, "*You changed my life.*"

Not because I was perfect. But because I showed up. I cared. I believed in them until they believed in themselves.

That's the quiet legacy of *priceless* leadership.

Priceless Leaders Shape Priceless Stories

If you take nothing else from this book, remember this: *Your leadership affects someone's sense of self-worth.*

The Priceless Leadership Model is more than a concept – it's a calling. When you see people as priceless, they begin to see themselves that way. And when they do, confidence grows. Competence follows. The cycle begins.

When you separate someone's behavior from their worth, you help them grow without shame. When you affirm their potential instead of labeling their mistakes, you help them write a better story about who they are.

And over time, the culture shifts. Not just because of policies or programs. But because you decided to lead differently.

Your Leadership Epitaph

If you had to sum up your leadership in one sentence – what would it be?

Here's mine:

"He helped people believe in themselves again."

What about you?

If that feels daunting, good. That means you care.

Try this: imagine someone who worked closely with you giving a eulogy – not for your life, but for your leadership. Close your eyes. Picture the room. What story are they telling – and what do you hope they say?

That legacy is written in how you lead today.

Back Where You Started... But Not the Same

Leadership isn't a straight line. It's a circle. So let's come back to where we began.

Remember when you were asked at the start of this journey to think about the best and worst leaders you've ever had?

Think back to those people now.

What made them unforgettable?

How did they make you feel?

What story did they leave behind in your heart – and your habits?

Now ask yourself...

• *What story will you leave behind?*

• *Are you becoming the kind of leader you once needed?*

• *Would your team describe you as someone who made them feel seen, valued, and, yes... priceless?*

You don't need a fancy title or a huge platform to leave a legacy.

You just need to choose, today, to lead with intention.

Knowledge fades. Titles change. But how you made people feel? That lasts.

This may be the final chapter – but it's not the end. It's the invitation to lead with worth. The movement begins when you decide to live it.

Ahead, you'll find practical tools and next steps to help you live out what you've learned – because leadership isn't about what you know. It's about what you do.

Want to keep growing?

Visit NationalALD.com to explore free leadership tools, host your own *Priceless!* book club, or bring the *Priceless! Workshop* to your team. You can also learn how to bring the *Priceless!* movement to your organization and help others lead with worth.

Let's take the next step – together.

Your legacy isn't just what you leave behind.

It's what you lead forward.

Chapter 12 Wrap-Up: Your Leadership Legacy

Key Takeaways

- Your leadership leaves a mark, whether you intend to or not.

- Legacy isn't just about achievements – it's about the people you've shaped and how they remember you.

- Living out the Priceless Leadership Model creates ripple effects beyond what you'll ever see.

- You don't have to wait to make an impact. Your legacy is being written now.

Reflection Questions

1. What do you want people to say about your leadership five years after you're gone?

2. Who are the leaders who shaped you – for better or worse – and what legacy did they leave?

3. What small, intentional actions can you begin today that align with the legacy you hope to leave?

Mini-Challenge

Write your legacy sentence. Sum up in one line the impact you hope your leadership will have. Keep it somewhere visible as a daily compass.

◈ The Priceless Punchline

Q: Why don't great leaders ever play hide and seek?
A: Because good luck hiding when your influence is everywhere.

Notes *(Use this space to capture your thoughts, reactions, or action steps from this chapter)*

_____

_____

_____

_____

_____

_____

_____

_____

_____

_____

_____

_____

_____

"Carve your name on hearts, not tombstones. A legacy is etched into the minds of others and the stories they share about you." – Shannon L. Alder

Acknowledgments

From the Heart of the Author

First and foremost, I want to thank God – the ultimate Author of this message and the One who gave me the heart to see people differently. Every story, insight, and lesson in this book is a reflection of His grace in my life. I've stumbled plenty, but His patience, presence, and purpose have never failed me.

If you've made it this far in the book, thank you. Not just for reading – but for caring. For choosing to lead in a way that sees people differently and treats them better. You're part of a growing movement now, and I'm honored to be walking this journey with you.

This book was born from decades of stories, mentors, lessons, and moments – some inspiring, some painful, all priceless. I couldn't have written a single word without the people who shaped me along the way.

I want to start by thanking my family.

To my wife, Christine – your love, your belief in me, and your daily example as a nurse caring for people in their most vulnerable moments inspire me more than words can say.

To my son, Alex – you've always carried wisdom beyond your years. Your strength and character have been a lighthouse for me – not just as your dad, but as a fellow traveler trying to live and lead well.

To my mom – you're sunshine in human form. Your optimism, your love of life, and your enduring belief in the good in others have shaped me more than you know.

To my brothers, Chris and Tim – you've taught me in your own ways what strength, wisdom, and perseverance look like.

To my dad – I miss you. You were my first leadership teacher. As Head of the Middle School at Berwick Academy, you showed me that real leadership isn't about authority – it's about kindness, presence, and how you treat people when no one's watching. Thank you for showing me what that looked like every day.

To my grandparents (Grammie and Gramps, Gammu and Papa), uncles and aunts, cousins, neighbors, and childhood chums – you filled my early years with love, laughter, and life lessons I carry to this day.

To the dear friends who've shaped me through every season – whether we met at Berwick, Johnson & Wales, or during long days and late nights in hotels, resorts, boardrooms, or training rooms filled with flip charts and big dreams – thank you. You've made the journey so much richer. While there's no way to mention everyone here, I'd be remiss if I didn't give a heartfelt shoutout to a few friends whose impact on my life and leadership has been especially profound: Justin, Alexi, Tony, JP, Wylie, Sara, Gary, Brent, Orlando, Eric, Pete, and Marco. You've been iron sharpening iron, laughter in the hard times, and faithful reminders of what true friendship looks like.

To the teachers who left a permanent mark on my heart – Mr. B, Mr. and Mrs. Payzant, Mrs. Towle, Mr. Hett, and Mr. Fletcher (to name a few) – thank you. You didn't just teach me; you believed in me. And that belief made all the difference.

To my pastors growing up – Reverend Barkley and Reverend Christensen – you both made church meaningful and alive for me. I didn't know it at the time, but the way you told stories, connected Scripture to life, and made faith feel relevant helped shape the communicator I am today. Thank you for that sacred gift.

To Governor John McKernan from the great state of Maine—thank you for letting a high school senior join your campaign and see leadership up close. I watched how you treated people behind the scenes, not just in front of cameras, and it left a lasting impression. We need more public servants like that – leaders who carry humility, heart, and integrity with them wherever they go.

To every team I've had the honor of leading – thank you. Whether we crossed paths in Hilton Head Island (Team Marriott and Hyatt Regency), Newport (Hotel Viking), New Haven (Holiday Inn), Milford (Marriott), Jamestown (Wyndham), Bermuda (St. Georges Club), the Berkshires (Wyndham), or these past 19 years in Orlando (Wyndham, Holiday Inn Club Vacations, and World Vision USA) – you shaped me as much as I ever hoped to shape you. Each place holds memories of laughter, challenges, lessons, and growth. I carry those seasons – and the people who made them special – with deep gratitude.

To the best bosses and mentors I've ever had – thank you for believing in people-first leadership and showing me how it's done. Some of you encouraged me, some challenged me, and others simply let me watch how you led. Barbara – I'll never forget how you sent me, without hesitation, to be with my dad when I needed it most. That one decision taught me more about leadership than most seminars ever could.

To the difficult bosses I've worked under – thank you, too. You showed me what not to do. Some of the most important leadership lessons come wrapped in frustration. They stick with you – and they shape you, too.

Marco (iLX Studios) – thank you for being my creative partner in this movement. You've brought my vision to life with brilliance, integrity, and friendship. I couldn't imagine a better teammate for this journey.

To those who read early drafts, submitted stories, or offered feedback – thank you for lending your voice. Your honesty, vulnerability, and stories gave this book its heartbeat.

And to my Great-grandmother Carpenter – thank you for passing down a story from the World War II days that has stayed with me since the day you shared it. I've never forgotten it, especially in dark times like these:

There is a brave pastor living in Germany today who throughout all the years has never once given the Nazi salute. He goes about the countryside where his name is a benediction, and for some unaccountable reason, violence seems loath to lay its heavy hands upon him. He is the Lord's servant, conscious of his commission, respected by all and perfectly frank in his disapproval of the way things have been going in the Fatherland for a decade.

Someone asked him how he had been able to survive all these years. His answer was simple:

"When I come home at night and find my home dark, I do not try to sweep out the darkness with a violent broom... I light a candle."

The world is so dark today because candles all over the world have, in the last generation, been going out. It is not because men love darkness; it was just that they were too self-indulgent to keep the tapers of love and fair-dealing aglow. And no matter how the present struggle comes out, the world will still be dark unless millions of people light candles again – or to speak plainly, unless those who believe in prayer begin to pray. Armies will have to march for many months, perhaps, but all the armies in the world will not drive out darkness.

The only way to overwhelm darkness... is for us all to light a candle.

In a world longing for better leadership, may we be the ones who light a candle. And may our influence, like those candles, burn quietly but brightly... leaving behind warmth, not just results. Thank you for believing in this message – and for helping carry it forward.

With deepest gratitude,
Scott Doggett

Epilogue:

Lead It Forward

A final word — and your next step as a Priceless leader.

You've reached the end of the book — but not the end of your impact.

The way you lead shapes the stories people carry for the rest of their lives. And when you lead like people are priceless, you build more than performance. You build trust. You build legacy. You build lives.

So where do you go from here?

➤ **Start by visiting: nationalald.com**

That's your next step in bringing *Priceless!* leadership to life. Whether you're looking to grow personally, invest in your team, or help others lead well, the National Academy of Leadership Development (NALD) is here to help. You'll find:

- Details on attending or hosting a Priceless! workshop (secular or faith-based)

- Options to get certified as a facilitator and teach *Priceless!* to others

- A growing library of free tools, including:

    o   AI-powered coaching resources

    o   Book club guides (secular or faith-based)

    o   Priceless leadership assessment tool

- o   Recommended articles, videos, and more
- And a way to contact us for speaking engagements, consulting services, or customized training experiences

So check out the site — because servant leadership was never meant to be a solo journey.

One More Challenge...

What's one thing you'll do in the next 30 days to lead like people are priceless?

Write it down. Share it with someone. Do it on purpose.

Because leadership is never neutral. And people are always... priceless.

So go now —

Lead forward. Lead with courage. Lead with heart.

Let's spark a Priceless leadership movement – together!

APPENDIX:

What Were They *Really* Thinking?
Why This Section Exists:

Throughout this book, you've encountered stories titled *"What Were They Thinking?"* – real snapshots of leadership moments. We invited you to step into someone else's shoes and reflect on what that person might have been feeling, thinking, or needing in that moment.

Now, here's your chance to peek behind the curtain. While we can't always know the full story, these glimpses offer a deeper look at the emotions, assumptions, and interpretations people carry – often silently – after a leadership moment.

Let these responses remind you that every interaction leaves a mark.

1. "The System That Broke Us" —Melissa R.
Chapter 2: The Cost of Performance-First Leadership

- **Thoughts:** "What was that?!", "Are we really going to get fired?", "I hate this!"

- **Feelings:** Disrespected, replaceable, anxious, frustrated.

- **Impact:** I disengaged almost immediately. I started avoiding my boss, mentally checked out, and began looking for a new job that same day. I left after about six months and brought two coworkers with me to a different call center.

2. "Invisible" — Chris M.
Chapter 3: The Priceless Leadership Model

- **Thoughts:** "Does this guy even know I exist?", "Why do I even try?". "How am I ever going to get ahead here is my boss doesn't even know who I am?"

- **Feelings:** Overlooked, unappreciated, frustrated, not valued.

- **Impact:** Chris stopped volunteering for projects outside his own scope. He is still there but has "quietly quit" (*as they say*) and is doing the bare minimum. He is currently looking for other opportunities outside that organization.

3. "The Breaking Point" — Tanya M.
Chapter 4: Priceless in Practice

- **Thoughts:** "Does anyone even notice what we're going through?", "Does anyone care?", "Why am I putting myself through this?"

- **Feelings:** Drained, hopeless, frustrated, defeated.

- **Impact:** Tanya kept her head down and did what she could, stopped speaking up in meetings, and because of the burnout, she ended up transferring to another hospital about 3 months after that moment.

4. "Just Get It Done" — David R.
Chapter 7: Scaling Servant Leadership

- **Thoughts:** "I am being set up for failure", "I am failing", "I just want to go back to my old job".

- **Feelings:** Lonely, frustrated, nervous.

- **Impact:** David ended up asking a peer for help with the situation and was very grateful but resented his boss, stopped recommending people come work there, and lost respect not just for his manager but for the company as a whole.

---

5. "The Fork in the Road" — Hannah B.
Chapter 10: The Ripple Effect

- **Thoughts:** "He knows who I am?!", "OMG...I can't believe it!", "I can't wait to keep working on this project!"

- **Feelings:** Seen, empowered, and energized.

- **Impact:** Hannah took on more initiative and volunteered to lead extra parts of the project, she stayed late several nights and didn't mind at all, and even asked about (and was eventually enrolled in) her company's emerging leader program after the project was done. She is committed to that organization and is a big advocate for their brand. (*She even tried to convince me to come work there lol*).

The Priceless Leadership Assessment

Instructions:
Rate yourself for each of the 12 traits below using this scale:

1 = **Rarely true of me**
2 = **Sometimes true**
3 = **Often true**
4 = **Consistently true**
5 = **A defining part of who I am as a leader**

Trait	Description	Score (1–5)
Empathy	I take time to understand others' perspectives and feelings.	_____
Humility	I admit mistakes, ask for feedback, and give others credit.	_____
Integrity	I do what's right, even when no one's watching.	_____
Compassion	I respond to others with care, patience, and kindness.	_____
Vision	I inspire others with a clear, meaningful direction.	_____
Wisdom	I apply discernment to tough choices and complex situations.	_____
Accountability	I hold myself and others responsible for commitments and behavior.	_____

Trait	Description	Score (1–5)
Discernment	I pause to pray, reflect, and seek insight before acting or advising.	_____
Service	I look for ways to support others – especially behind the scenes.	_____
Empowerment	I equip and trust others to take ownership and grow.	_____
Stewardship	I manage time, resources, and influence in ways that honor others.	_____
Courage	I speak the truth in love and make hard decisions with care.	_____

Add up your scores for each domain below to discover your unique leadership profile:

- **Heart** (Empathy, Humility, Integrity, Compassion): _____

- **Head** (Vision, Wisdom, Accountability, Discernment): _____

- **Hands** (Service, Empowerment, Stewardship, Courage): _____

My Priceless Leadership Development Plan

Instructions:

Choose one trait from the Priceless Leadership Assessment that you want to strengthen. Then use the **70-20-10** model to build a practical development plan:

- **70%** – Learn by doing (real-life application)
- **20%** – Learn with or from others (coaching, feedback, mentoring)
- **10%** – Learn through study (books, courses, reflection)

Trait I'm Focusing On:

_____

_____

_____

_____

_____

_____

Why I Chose This Trait:

_____

_____

_____

70% – Learn by Doing (Practice ideas you can apply in your current role):

_____

_____

_____

_____

_____

20% – Learn with or from Others (*People who can coach, mentor, or offer feedback*):

_____

_____

_____

_____

_____

10% – Learn through Study (*Resources that will help me grow in this trait*):

_____

_____

_____

_____

_____

How I'll Measure Progress *(What growth will look like, and how you will track it over time):*

_____

_____

_____

_____

_____

_____

Footnotes

1. Robert K. Greenleaf, *The Servant as Leader* (Indianapolis: Greenleaf Center, 1970).

2. James L. Heskett, W. Earl Sasser Jr., and Leonard A. Schlesinger, *The Service Profit Chain* (New York: Free Press, 1997).

3. James L. Heskett, W. Earl Sasser Jr., and Leonard A. Schlesinger, *The Service Profit Chain* (New York: Free Press, 1997).

4. John D. Rockefeller, *Random Reminiscences of Men and Events* (New York: Doubleday, 1909).

5. Attributed to Theodore Roosevelt; original source uncertain but widely cited.

6. Maya Angelou, *Phenomenal Woman* (New York: Random House, 1995).

7. Robert K. Greenleaf, *The Servant as Leader* (Indianapolis: Greenleaf Center, 1970).

8. Robert K. Greenleaf, *The Servant as Leader* (Indianapolis: Greenleaf Center, 1970).

9. Chick-fil-A, "Our Commitment to People First," https://www.chick-fil-a.com.

10. James L. Heskett, W. Earl Sasser Jr., and Leonard A. Schlesinger, *The Service Profit Chain* (New York: Free Press, 1997).

11. TDIndustries, "About TDIndustries: Our Culture and Servant Leadership," https://www.tdindustries.com.

12. TDIndustries, "About TDIndustries: Our Culture and Servant Leadership," https://www.tdindustries.com.

13. Robert K. Greenleaf, *The Servant as Leader* (Indianapolis: Greenleaf Center, 1970).

14. TDIndustries, "About TDIndustries: Our Culture and Servant Leadership," https://www.tdindustries.com.

15. Robert K. Greenleaf, *The Servant as Leader* (Indianapolis: Greenleaf Center, 1970).

16. Robert K. Greenleaf, *The Servant as Leader* (Indianapolis: Greenleaf Center, 1970).

17. James L. Heskett, W. Earl Sasser Jr., and Leonard A. Schlesinger, *The Service Profit Chain* (New York: Free Press, 1997).

18. James L. Heskett, W. Earl Sasser Jr., and Leonard A. Schlesinger, *The Service Profit Chain* (New York: Free Press, 1997).

19. James L. Heskett, W. Earl Sasser Jr., and Leonard A. Schlesinger, *The Service Profit Chain* (New York: Free Press, 1997).

20. James L. Heskett, W. Earl Sasser Jr., and Leonard A. Schlesinger, *The Service Profit Chain* (New York: Free Press, 1997).

21. James L. Heskett, W. Earl Sasser Jr., and Leonard A. Schlesinger, *The Service Profit Chain* (New York: Free Press, 1997).

22. James L. Heskett, W. Earl Sasser Jr., and Leonard A. Schlesinger, *The Service Profit Chain* (New York: Free Press, 1997).

23. James L. Heskett, W. Earl Sasser Jr., and Leonard A. Schlesinger, *The Service Profit Chain* (New York: Free Press, 1997).

24. Chick-fil-A, "Our Commitment to People First," https://www.chick-fil-a.com.

25. Chick-fil-A, "Our Commitment to People First," https://www.chick-fil-a.com.

26. Chick-fil-A, "Our Commitment to People First," https://www.chick-fil-a.com.

27. Chick-fil-A, "Our Commitment to People First," https://www.chick-fil-a.com.

28. Chick-fil-A, "Our Commitment to People First," https://www.chick-fil-a.com.

29. Chick-fil-A, "Our Commitment to People First," https://www.chick-fil-a.com.

30. Chick-fil-A, "Our Commitment to People First," https://www.chick-fil-a.com.

31. Chick-fil-A, "Our Commitment to People First," https://www.chick-fil-a.com.

32. James L. Heskett, W. Earl Sasser Jr., and Leonard A. Schlesinger, *The Service Profit Chain* (New York: Free Press, 1997).

33. James L. Heskett, W. Earl Sasser Jr., and Leonard A. Schlesinger, *The Service Profit Chain* (New York: Free Press, 1997).

34. James L. Heskett, W. Earl Sasser Jr., and Leonard A. Schlesinger, *The Service Profit Chain* (New York: Free Press, 1997).

35. James L. Heskett, W. Earl Sasser Jr., and Leonard A. Schlesinger, *The Service Profit Chain* (New York: Free Press, 1997).

36. Brené Brown, "The Power of Vulnerability," TEDxHouston, 2010, https://www.ted.com/talks/brene_brown_on_vulnerability.

37. James C. Hunter, *The Servant* (New York: Crown Business, 1998).

38. The Container Store, "Leadership and Culture," https://www.containerstore.com.

39. The Container Store, "Leadership and Culture," https://www.containerstore.com.

40. The Container Store, "Leadership and Culture," https://www.containerstore.com.

41. The Container Store, "Leadership and Culture," https://www.containerstore.com.

42. The Container Store, "Leadership and Culture," https://www.containerstore.com.

43. The Container Store, "Leadership and Culture," https://www.containerstore.com.

44. Maya Angelou, *Phenomenal Woman* (New York: Random House, 1995).

Bibliography

Angelou, Maya. *Phenomenal Woman: Four Poems Celebrating Women*. New York: Random House, 1995.

American Psychological Association. "Work and Well-Being Survey Results, 2024." APA.org. https://www.apa.org.

Brown, Brené. *Dare to Lead: Brave Work. Tough Conversations. Whole Hearts.* New York: Random House, 2018.

Brown, Brené. "The Power of Vulnerability." TEDxHouston, June 2010. https://www.ted.com/talks/brene_brown_on_vulnerability.

Foley, James W. "Drop a Pebble in the Water." *The Speaker*, 1912.

Firestone, Harvey S. *Men and Rubber: The Story of Business*. New York: Doubleday, Page & Co., 1926.

Greenleaf, Robert K. *The Servant as Leader*. Indianapolis: Greenleaf Center for Servant Leadership, 1970.

Hall, Kevin. *Aspire: Discovering Your Purpose Through the Power of Words*. New York: HarperCollins, 2010.

Heskett, James L., W. Earl Sasser Jr., and Leonard A. Schlesinger. *The Service Profit Chain: How Leading Companies Link Profit and Growth to Loyalty, Satisfaction, and Value*. New York: Free Press, 1997.

Hunter, James C. *The Servant: A Simple Story About the True Essence of Leadership*. New York: Crown Business, 1998.

Rockefeller, John D. *Random Reminiscences of Men and Events*. New York: Doubleday, Page & Co., 1909.

Sinek, Simon. *Start with Why: How Great Leaders Inspire Everyone to Take Action*. New York: Portfolio, 2009.

Southwest Airlines. "Our Purpose and Vision." https://www.southwest.com.

TDIndustries. "About TDIndustries: Our Culture and Servant Leadership." https://www.tdindustries.com.

The Container Store. "Leadership and Culture." https://www.containerstore.com.

Chick-fil-A. "Our Commitment to People First." https://www.chick-fil-a.com.

www.ingramcontent.com/pod-product-compliance
Lightning Source LLC
Chambersburg PA
CBHW051624120626
46551CB00014B/1929